DUE DATE

THE
BAPTISTS

THE BAPTISTS

Anne Devereaux Jordan
and
J. M. Stifle

HIPPOCRENE BOOKS
New York

For information, address: Hippocrene Books, Inc.,
171 Madison Avenue, New York, NY 10016.

Library of Congress Cataloging-in-Publication Data

Jordan, Anne Devereaux.
  The Baptists / Anne Devereaux Jordan and J.M. Stifle.
    p.   cm.
  Includes bibliographical references.
  ISBN 0-87052-784-3
  1. Baptists.   I. Stifle, J. M.   II. Title.
  BX6331.2.J63   1990
  286'.09—dc20   89-77152
                                                         CIP

Editorial development, design and production by
Combined Books, Inc.
26 Summit Grove Ave., Suite 207,
Bryn Mawr, PA 19010
(215) 527-9276

Printed in the United States of America.

*Jacket photo courtesy of the State Historical Society of
Wisconsin.*

For Mary, and, of course, for David.
　　　　　　—Anne D. Jordan

For Elva, Charlie, and Dorothy,
　　　　　whose
faith has sustained them.
　　　　　　—J. M. Stifle

Contents

Acknowledgments   x
Introduction   xi

Chapter I
Troubled Times: The Reformation   1

Chapter II
The Spirit of the Reformation: Separatists and
Baptists   9

Chapter III
Liberty and Strife: The Early Baptists   19

Chapter IV
"A Lively Experiment": The Early Baptists in New
England   27

Chapter V
"Agreement and Confederation"   37

Chapter VI
The Great Awakening   43

Chapter VII
"Liberty and Toleration"   55

Chapter VIII
"A Heavenly Confusion": The Great Revival   65

Chapter IX
"Spreading Evangelical Truth": The Baptist
Missionary Movement   75

Chapter X
Spreading the Word: Education and
Publication   85

Chapter XI
Brother Against Brother: Splits and
Schisms   93

Chapter XII
"Shall We Gather at the River?": The Modern Baptist
Conventions   107

Chapter XIII
The Twentieth Century: Science, Modernism and
"That Old Time Religion"   119

Chapter XIV
   "A Return to Normalcy"?   135

Chapter XV
   The Electronic Revival   147

Appendix: Baptist Principles   161

Bibliography   163

Index   169

Acknowledgments

We would like to thank the following persons and organizations for providing helpful information regarding Baptist history: Stan L. Hastey, Director of Information Services, Baptist Joint Committee on Public Affairs; Harold C. Bennett, Executive Secretary-Treasurer, and Lynn E. May, Executive Director-Treasurer, The Historical Commission, Southern Baptist Convention; Glen O. Spence, Executive Secretary, General Association of General Baptists; Ruby J. Burke, Communications Department, Baptist World Alliance; Marie Schultz, Office of the Board of Trustees, Baptist General Conference; O. J. Malloy, Jr., General Secretary, Progressive National Baptist Convention, Inc.; and Robert C. Campbell, General Secretary, and Patricia Schlosser, Administrative Assistant, Office of the General Secretary, American Baptist Churches in the U.S.A., and the State Historical Society of Wisconsin for permission to use the photograph on the jacket.

Introduction

ON JANUARY 12, 1976, BAPTISTS FROM ALL OVER THE
United States and Canada gathered in Washington,
D.C., for a National Bicentennial Convocation: "Baptists and the American Experience." In the introduction to the convocation proceedings, James Wood,
Director of the Baptist Joint Committee on Public Affairs, summed up the Baptist experience in America:

> In less than 200 years since the founding of the
> nation, Baptists have moved from the position of a
> persecuted and disinherited sect to the largest
> Protestant denomination in America, comprising
> approximately one-seventh of the total population.
> In many parts of the country, Baptists have become
> socially established as the dominant and largest
> religious community. Far from being regarded as
> radicals or revolutionaries, as they were in seventeenth-century England and America, Baptists to-

day are generally widely regarded as politically and socially conservative, defenders of the status quo.

Baptists have indeed come a long way from their humble origins in 1609 as a small band of English religious exiles in Amsterdam, Holland. Today there are over 35 million Baptists worldwide.

Nine-tenths of the world's Baptists live in the United States, most belonging to one of the 20 leading Baptist conventions, of which the Southern Baptist Convention is the largest. In 1800, Baptists accounted for less than two percent of the total American population. Since that time the Baptist denomination has grown at a rate five times that of the general population. Their numbers increased 243 percent in the first half of the twentieth century alone. This phenomenal growth led a Methodist bishop to quip, "If the present rate of growth continues, there would be more . . . Baptists than people by the year 2015."

Today the denomination is second only to the Roman Catholic Church in size, and it is twice the size of the second-largest Protestant denomination in America, the Methodist church.

The Baptist presence in America has greatly enriched our national heritage and has enriched countries throughout the world. The devotion of the Baptist founding fathers to the principles of democracy, individual freedom, and religious and civil liberty helped mold the national consciousness of the United States and shape our system of government. The Rev. George W. Truett, a notable Baptist preacher of the early twentieth century, eloquently outlined these ideals in an address delivered from the steps of the White House on May 6, 1920:

> Baptists have one consistent record concerning liberty throughout their long and eventful history. . . . They have forever been the unwavering champions of liberty, both religious and civil. Their contention now is, and has been, and, please God must ever be, that it is the natural and fundamental and indefeasible right of every human being to worship God or not, according to the dictates of his conscience, and, as long as he does not infringe upon the rights of others, he is to be held accountable alone to God for all religious beliefs and practices. Our contention is not for mere toleration, but for absolute liberty. . . . It is the consistent and insistent contention of our Baptist people, always and everywhere, that religion must be forever voluntary and uncoerced, and that it is not the prerogative of any power, whether civil or ecclesiastical, to compel men to conform to any religious creed or form of worship, or to pay taxes for the support of a religious organization to which they do not belong and in which they do not believe. God wants free worshippers and no other king.

Similarly, in his 1976 inaugural speech, our first Southern Baptist president, Jimmy Carter, paid tribute to the ideals of his Baptist forebears: "Ours was the first society openly to define itself in terms of both spirituality and of human liberty. It is that unique self-definition which has given us an exceptional appeal."

The president went on to call for a "resurgent commitment to the basic principles of our nation . . . human rights . . . personal liberty . . . and a spirit of individual sacrifice for the common good."

It was the search for principles such as these that not only brought our nation together, but that, in the perilous times of the seventeenth century, also drew a small band of believers together to establish the Baptist community that has spread throughout the world today.

I

Troubled Times: The Reformation

SIXTEENTH-CENTURY EUROPE WAS A CONTINENT obscured by the clouds of hardship and fear. Peasants labored from dawn to dusk to scrape the barest of existences from the soil while their rulers waged war both internally and beyond their countries' borders. Trading ships from the East unwittingly had transported diseased rats carrying the Black Death, a plague that swept across Europe like a flood, killing lowborn and highborn alike and decimating entire towns. Daily life for the peasant was a continuous battle with the threats of starvation, war, disease, superstition, and ignorance.

1

On a larger scale, however, social, political, and economic changes were in the air. By the start of the seventeenth century, Europe and England both were laboring against the chains of the dying feudal system and the Roman Catholic Church, and were rebelling against the old superstitions and fears.

The dawn of the seventeenth century revealed a Europe that was largely rural. Agriculture was, as it had been for centuries, the economic mainstay of the various principalities and countries. But with a difference. The abuses of the feudal system had given rise to bloody revolts throughout Europe during the previous century. Most peasants were no longer literal slaves to their lords. There were now both free and tenant farmers. Although both were still heavily burdened by taxes and, for the tenant, services to his lord, the owner of his land, life was no longer the unrewarded, brutish existence it had been.

Similar change was occurring among the lay rulers and the religious rulers of Europe. The Holy Roman Empire and its ruler, the pope, had been the unifying political and religious force for centuries. But the grip of the empire had been weakened internally by dissenting factions, and enervated externally by recurring invasions from the north. Many local rulers took the opportunity to wrest leadership from Rome, creating a separation of church and state. Where the Church still held sway, the pope found himself relying more heavily on local bishops to take care of the day-to-day routine of tending the empire. Without close supervision from Rome, however, these same bishops often took advantage of their increased authority to set themselves up as petty despots, increasing dissatisfaction with the Roman Catholic Church.

One source of dissatisfaction was the economic burden the Church placed on its followers. Annually, the Church demanded tribute from kings and fees from its bishops when they were appointed. Taxes were levied for the building of churches and other projects. But the source of income that ultimately was to cause the greatest dissension was the selling of indulgences. Indulgences were sold for the remission of the punishment for sins. The pentitent paid for indulgences in cash. Originally indulgences were issued only in special cases as one form of penance. But by the seventeenth century, they were issued generally and were a lucrative source of income and subject, naturally, to abuse.

The issue of indulgences, as well as other abuses by the Church, gave rise to a call for reform. The Church, many felt, was forgetting its spiritual mission for the base coin offered by this world. As Erasmus (1466-1536) had written earlier, "Truly the yoke of Christ would be sweet, and His burdens light, if petty human institutions added nothing to what He Himself imposed. He commanded us nothing save love for one another."

Those calling for reform of the Roman Catholic Church fell into one of three catagories.

There were spiritual reformers, who deplored worldly pursuits and advocated programs of piety and austerity. There were advocates of the conciliar theory, who wished to see an ecumenical council reform the Church institutionally. Finally, there were the humanists, who believed that knowledge of the Bible would restore the purity that had characterized the early Church.[1]

At the time, these various factions for reform little touched a young man who was preoccupied with carrying out his priestly duties in Wittenberg in what is now Germany. Yet, ultimately, Martin Luther would be the man to lead what has become known as the Reformation and provide the foundation upon which the various Protestant denominations we have today would be built.

November 11 was Saint Martin's Day in the little town of Eisleban in Saxony, one of the larger principalities of the Holy Roman Empire. Saint Martin was the patron saint of drinking and merriment and his day was one of celebration, especially for Hans and Margaret Luther, whose second son was born on Saint Martin's Eve in 1483. In honor of the saint, they named their new son Martin.

Martin Luther's father, Hans, was a man whose own life reflected the changing nature of society at that time. Born a peasant, he had moved to Eisleban, where he worked as a copper miner. After some years of working and saving, he moved to Mansfeld and, borrowing some money, leased a small smelting furnace.[2] He had made the transition from the land to entrepreneur as so many were doing throughout Europe.

[1] Edith Simon and the editors of Time-Life Books, *The Reformation* (Alexandria, Va.: Time-Life Books, 1966), P. 36.
  [2] *Ibid.,* p. 14

Stubborn and dour, Hans wished for Martin to better himself even more than he had and ordered him to study law. After a few months, however, Martin became dissatisfied with his studies and, much to his father's disappointment, entered the Augustinian cloister at Erfurt.

Martin Luther began his monastic studies in 1505 at the age of 21. Erfurt was a monastery known for its austere regimen, and Martin Luther followed this with zeal and devotion. As he later wrote, "If ever a monk got to heaven by his monkery, I would have made it. All my brothers in the monastery will testify that had I gone on with it I would have killed myself with vigils, prayers, reading, and other works." Both his zeal and his intelligence were apparent to his superiors, and they eventually sent him to study at the University of Wittenberg. After two years of studying and teaching, he was sent to accompany a senior friar to Rome on a diplomatic mission, a trip that was to be significant for Luther.

Martin Luther looked at Rome and found beauty in its architecture and art and kindliness in its people, but he also saw the pride and the greed, the pomp and the luxury to which the Church had fallen prey. His mission in Rome completed, he returned to Wittenberg. However, for Luther, the seeds of dissatisfaction had been sown. In that same year (1511) one of Luther's professors exclaimed prophetically

This monk will confuse all the doctors. He will start a new religion and reform the whole Roman Church, for he bases his theology on the writings of the Prophets and the Apostles. He stands on the words of Christ, which no philosophy or sophistry

can upset or oppose, be it that of the Scotists, the
Albertists [or] the Thomists.

A year later Luther received his degree from Wittenberg
and embarked on his career of teaching and preaching.

During the years that followed, Luther's dissatisfaction with the Church grew. He longed to strip away all
the trappings of wealth and power and restore to the
Church the basic teachings of Christian love and faith.
He gradually came to believe that man's salvation was
determined by God alone. Those who were redeemed
received the gift of faith in Christ. Through studying the
Bible, Luther found in Paul's letters what he felt was an
essential idea the Church should strive to teach: "The
just shall live by faith." "Finally," Luther wrote, "God
had mercy on me and I began to understand that the
righteousness of God is that gift of God by which a
righteous man lives, namely, faith." This gift was given
freely by God to those He selected; it could not be
earned, begged, or most importantly, bought. Luther
had discovered what has become known as the doctrine of predestination.

Excited by this idea, Luther began to speak out
against the indulgence-selling priests and to preach his
doctrine of salvation through God-given grace alone,
drawing the anger of Church authorities. They saw his
teachings as a direct threat to the stability of the
Church. In August of 1520 Luther published his *Address to the Christian Nobility of the German Nation*,
which called for secular reform of the Church. This was
followed by a flood of other books and pamphlets that
often were burned by public officials. In retaliation
Luther burned the *Canon Law*, the sacred document

recording the laws of the Church, at Wittenberg on December 10, 1520. He promptly was excommunicated from the Church. The only step that remained was for the Church to declare Luther an outlaw. Steps were taken at the Diet of Worms to achieve this, and in 1521, the Edict of Worms named Martin Luther an outlaw and forced him into hiding for a number of years.

Although Luther was known in the Church and throughout the land as an outlaw, the Edict failed to quell the reformation Luther had championed. Change had begun and could not be stopped; the Holy Roman Empire was in its death throes. The Roman Catholic Church would survive, but its hold on all facets of life, its vast properties—its empire—was lost.

II

The Spirit of the Reformation: Separatists and Baptists

IN HIS EFFORTS TO REFORM THE CHURCH, LUTHER URGED doing away with or simplifying many church rituals and advocated a number of revolutionary concepts regarding man's relationship to God and the church and the church's relationship to society. These ideas would lay the groundwork for all the Protestant denominations that would emerge from the Reformation.

The most far-reaching and radical of Luther's ideas were, of course, the concept of predestination and a church made up of God's chosen. For Luther, salvation was based not on man's worldly efforts, but on complete trust in God's promise. Luther saw man as a sinner, but a forgiven sinner because of the new relationship achieved with God through Jesus Christ. If one had faith, one was saved. He found his justification for this belief in Galatians 3:11-12: "he shall gain life who is justified through faith." Since church membership was reserved for the "elect"—those who were saved—Luther taught that all church members should be equal. No priest or bishop should stand higher in the eyes of God than the laity. He said, "Our baptism consecrates us all without exception and makes us all priests."

Luther also rejected all but two of the Catholic Church's seven sacraments. He retained only baptism and the Eucharist (Communion) because these were the only sacraments, according to the Bible, introduced by Christ while he was on earth. These sacraments were to be performed simply, however, without the ceremony and ritual that had been introduced since the age of the Apostles.

Luther also advocated the establishment of local state churches free from a centralized authority such as Rome's, and even more radical, he advocated the separation of religious and political authority within the state.

A revolution was under way. But why was Luther's voice to be heard so much more strongly when there existed others crying for reform? Partly it was the age; the times were ripe for change at the moment Luther spoke. His voice spoke to the people, to scholars, to other dissatisfied clergy. When he spoke, or wrote, it was eloquent and forceful. Many heard and acted, taking up the cause of reform and expanding on it. There were, of course, those who were not as sincere as Luther who used his ideas for their personal gain. But whatever their motives, the legions of reformers who followed Luther permanently changed the direction of religious history and brought to an end Rome's spiritual and political hold over the Western world.

The Reformation gave rise to myriad splinter groups and denominations in Europe and England. The Baptists were one such group, and although not directly related to Luther, Calvin, Knox, or Zwingli, the great reformers of the age, they shared Luther's desire for independence and valued many of the same qualities and ideas Luther did. They, too, wanted freedom from the established church and freedom from governmental interference. The early Baptists sought freedom to read and interpret the Scriptures according to their own belief in God, and they held a strong belief in adult believer's baptism rather than infant baptism. Although the Baptists often are thought to be linked to the early Anabaptists because of their views on adult baptism, most Baptist historians disavow this idea.

The roots of the Baptists start in England, growing out of the Puritan and Separatist movements. The first Baptists were those who wished for reform or to separate from the established church in England whether it was the Roman Catholic Church or the Church of England. The leading figure among this group was John Smyth (?-1612), an Anglican preacher who renounced the episcopacy in the early seventeenth century while speaking at Lincoln Cathedral. He was removed by church authorities and became pastor to a small group of Separatists, a group that eventually would form the first Baptist church.

In the early part of the sixteenth century, King Henry VIII had separated the English church from the Roman Catholic Church. He did so largely for personal and political reasons rather than because of liturgical differences. The only aspect of the Roman Church that Henry VIII utterly rejected was the Pope's claim to sovereignty over the entire church. Soon after, the Separatists called for more extreme measures. They rejected the Church of England because they felt it was still too much like the Catholic Church to be the true church. Their views were considered subversive by both the church and the state, and members were forced to conduct their meetings underground for fear of persecution by the established church authorities, led by the English monarch.

Robert Browne (1550?–1633), known as "Trouble Church Browne" for his radical views, is credited with organizing the first Separatist congregation in 1581. His views were influenced by the Dutch Anabaptists, another reform group of the time with whom he had come into contact. The Separatists (or "Brownists") did not regard infant baptism as a sacrament, but they did advocate it as a symbolic act of dedicating children to God and the church. They also believed that the church was made up of independent communities of "saints" who had made an agreement, or covenant, with God and one another to live and work together in Christian fellowship. Several other reform groups adopted the idea of the covenant—the most well-known in America being the ratification among the so-called Mayflower Church, bound for the New World in 1620.

The Separatists eventually were hounded out of England by the passage of a number of laws intended to make them conform to the Church of England. They fled to Amsterdam, where they found refuge, and where in 1606 John Smyth and his congregation likewise sought the freedom to practice their religion.

John Smyth's life reflects the path many Anglicans followed at that time. As a child Smyth was raised in a home that strongly followed the tenets of the Church of England, and it was only natural that as an adult he would choose to become a preacher. He studied at Cambridge and while there met Francis Johnson, who also would move from Anglican beliefs to those of the Separatists. Smyth's views even as a student were too radical for the staid Anglicans. Upon his graduation in 1602, when he delivered his controversial sermon, he was dismissed from his position in the ministry. After practicing medicine for a short time, Smyth joined with the Separatists and assumed the pastorate at Gainsborough in Nottinghamshire.

The ascension of King James I, who ruled England from 1603 to 1625, began a new round of persecution against those who called for religious reform. King James swore, "I will make them conform themselves, or I will have them out of the land."

Under James I, the Anabaptists (from whom the Mennonites and Amish are descended), the Puritans (who fled to America), and the Separatists all were forced to leave England. When the Anglican ministry heard of John Smyth's congregation at Gainsborough, persecution was focused on them, and in 1607, the group was

forced to flee to Amsterdam, where there already existed a sizeable community of Separatist exiles.

Not long after his arrival in Amsterdam, Smyth began to fall out with the Separatist community there,
questioning some of the tenets upon which their group
was based. After intensively studying the Bible, Smyth
came to the conclusion that the officers of a true
church should be confined to bishops and deacons,
and these only as elected by the members of a congregation and only after fasting and prayer. By electing
such officers, however, a congregation did not surrender any of its power to them. In Smyth's mind every
believer was a minister capable of administering the
sacraments and preaching the gospel. In short, Smyth
maintained that each congregation, not its officers or
any church hierarchy, held the highest authority in the
church next to God. He published these opinions in his
*Principles and Inferences Concerning the Visible
Church* (1607). Smyth also felt that there should be no
psalm-singing or sermon-reading in the church. It was
his views on infant baptism, however, that led to his
final break with the Separatists.

While in Amsterdam, Smyth was introduced to Ana-
baptist teachings through the Mennonite community
there, the Waterlander Mennonites. Smyth became convinced that infant baptism scripturally was invalid,
and that "believer's baptism"—the baptism of those
who have made a personal covenant with God—was
the true Christian sacrament. As Smyth wrote of his
new conviction, baptism

is not washing with water: but it is the baptism of
the Spirit, the confession of the mouth, and the

washing with water: how then can any man without great folly wash with water which is the least artd last of baptism, one that is not baptized with the Spirit and cannot confess with the mouth.

In his *The Character of the Beast* (1609), Smyth expounded on this view and declared that the baptisms of established churches were not valid.

In 1609 Smyth gathered a group of his followers together, 36 in all, and after a confession of faith, baptized himself and then Thomas Helwys and the others. He justified this audacious move, saying, "There is good warrant for a man churching himself. For two men singly are no church; so may two men put baptism upon themselves." A single person cannot constitute a church but two together can and so may also assume the right to baptize themselves. With this ceremony the Baptist movement is said to have begun.

As with many other dissenting sects before and after them, Baptists were given their name by those who opposed them. Richard Bernard, a member of the Amsterdam Separatist community, referred to Smyth as a "Se-Baptist." The first Baptists preferred to call themselves "Baptized Believers" or "Christians Baptized on Profession of Their Faith." Those names proved too cumbersome, however, and the more popular term "Baptist" soon gained widespread acceptance.

Not long after the formation of his group of "Baptists," Smyth's views again underwent a change. He came more and more under the influence of Jan Munter, the leader of the Waterlander Mennonites in Amsterdam, and eventually became convinced that he had made a serious error in baptizing himself and his followers. As Smyth's ideas evolved, a number of his original group came to disagree with his new views and, in 1611, withdrew to form a separate group led by Thomas Helwys. When Smyth petitioned to join the Mennonite church, Helwys' group excommunicated Smyth, and declared themselves the "true church," and returned to England. Smyth, continuing to defend himself to the end, died in Holland in August of 1616.

Thomas Helwys (1550?–1616) was a gentleman and a practicing lawyer when he joined John Smyth's Gainsborough church around 1605. He threw open his home, Broxtowe Hall, to his new fellow Separatists and contributed a great deal of financial support to the cause. In 1606 he followed Smyth to Amsterdam. His family did not escape the persecution from which Helwys had fled, however, and his wife, Joan, was arrested and imprisoned at York Castle. The King seized Helwys's assets and Broxtowe Hall.

Helwys continued his financial support of the Separatist community in Amsterdam and wholly supported John Smyth in his movement away from the Separatists until Smyth attempted to join the newly formed Baptists with the Waterlander Mennonites. The break with Smyth seemed to galvanize Helwys and he determined to return to England for two reasons. First, he wished to spread the word of Baptists because "thousands of ignorant souls in our country were perishing for lack of instruction." Second, he wished to champion the right of religious freedom. In his *A Short Declaration of the Mistery of Iniquity* (1612), he defended his position, saying,

Let the King judge, if it is not most equal that men should choose their religion themselves, seeing they only must stand themselves before the judgment seat of God to answer for themselves. . . . We profess and teach that in all earthly things the King's power is to be submitted unto, and in heavenly or spiritual things, if the King or any in authority under him shall exercise their power against any, they are not to resist by any way or means, although it were in their power, but rather to submit their lives as Christ and his disciples did and yet keep their consciences to God.[1]

Helwys and his congregation established their church at Spitalfields near London in 1612, becoming the first Baptist congregation in England. They adhered to the doctrine of general atonement (that Christ died for all). This was in direct opposition to the Calvinist doctrine of limited atonement or salvation only for God's elect, the principle Martin Luther had espoused (predestination) and that a majority of Protestants believed at the time.

It was Helwys's campaign for religious liberty, however, that brought about his death. In the inscription to his book *A Short Declaration of the Mistery of Iniquity*, he had written, "The King is a mortall man and not God, therefore hath no power over y immortall soules of his subjects to make lawes and ordinances for them to set spiritual Lords over them." This was a slap in the face for King James I. Helwys was imprisoned at Newgate and had died by 1616, when the leadership of the first Baptist church in England passed to his friend John Murton.

[1] Thomas Armitage, *A History of the Baptists*, (New York: Bryan, Taylor and Co., 1887), p. 455.

Although Thomas Helwys died just as the Baptist denomination was beginning, he, like John Smyth, left his mark upon it. His demands for religious liberty signaled the end of the medieval synthesis of a Christian state and are reflected both in the staunch independence of the Baptists even today and in the insistence that "God alone is Lord of the conscience."

III

Liberty and Strife: The Early Baptists

ALTHOUGH THOMAS HELWYS DIED BEFORE HE COULD SEE his efforts toward liberty bear fruit, his ideas lived on. They had been incorporated in a doctrinal statement, called a Confession of Faith, drawn up by the General Baptists in 1612. The confession contains the first modern demand by a religious body for freedom of conscience and the separation of church and state. Article 84 of the confession reads:

> That the magistrate is not by virtue of his office to meddle with religion or matters of conscience, to force or compel men to this or that form of re-

ligion, or doctrine: but to leave the Christian religion free to every man's conscience, and to handle only civil transgressions, . . . injuries and wrongs against men . . . for Christ only is the King, and lawgiver of the Church and conscience.

Because of the statements contained in this Confession of Faith and the various beliefs held by the General Baptists, they were considered a radical sect and persecuted by both the state and other religions. But they were growing slowly. By 1626 there were five General Baptist congregations with a total of 150 members in England. It was not until after the English civil wars (1640–1650), though, that there would be a significant increase in the number of General Baptists in England. By that time, however, they would be overshadowed by yet another group of Baptists known as the Particular Baptists.

The Calvinistic or Particular Baptists, so-called for their belief in the strict predestination doctrine of limited atonement, tended to come from a higher social level and hold more conservative views than the General Baptists. The first Particular church is said to have grown out of a London Separatist congregation around 1616, and, during its early years, sought to clarify the issue of baptism. Like the General Baptists, members of the Particular Baptists concluded that infant baptism was not in accordance with the Bible and adopted the idea of a "believer's" baptism (adult baptism). A few years later, after consultation with Dutch Collegiants, they reached a similar conclusion regarding the proper mode of baptism. The practice of immersion is the mode of baptism described in the New Testament; John the Baptist immersed his converts in the Jordan River and Christ himself was baptized by immersion. The Particular Baptists quickly adopted this method of baptism. The idea of immersion was one the General Baptists had not thought of but, by the 1640s, they, too, adopted the practice of immersion.

In 1644, when they drew up their Confession of Faith in London, the Particular Baptists numbered over 50 members in seven congregations. Their Calvinistic doctrine had a wider appeal among English Protestants than did the Arminianism (belief in the salvation of all) of the General Baptists. The Particular Baptists soon became the dominant group among English Baptists.

The London Confession of Faith, issued in 1644, helped in the delineation of the Baptist identity and was an attempt to link Baptists with established English Protestantism. Previous to the London Confession, each congregation was totally autonomous. In the London Confession, however, the Baptist leaders, while reinforcing the independence of each congregation—each was "a compact and knit city in itself"—also recognized the usefulness of joining together. The London Confession stated that it was helpful for the congregations "by all means convenient to have the counsel and help of one another in all needful affairs of the Church." This idea, reflected in later confessions by both English and American groups, reinforced the idea of denominationalism and allowed Baptists the opportunity for national and international organization. From this early, loose association among congregations grew formal arrangements of unity. In 1689 a General Assembly of Particular Baptists was organized. Although it lacked the power to heavily influence its member churches, who feared for their local church autonomy, it was a means by which the various Particular congregations could join to work together.

Both the General and Particular Baptists evangelized actively throughout the British Isles, and their numbers steadily grew. By 1655 there were about 79 General Baptist churches and 96 Particular Baptist churches— although their position always was precarious, their fortunes shifting according to who occupied the English throne. It was during the English civil wars and the Commonwealth period (1640–1660) that the Baptists flourished and won their first significant battles for religious liberty.

Baptists throughout England saw Oliver Cromwell's battle against the authority of the English monarchy as a fight for religious as well as civil liberty, and they gave Cromwell their wholehearted support. The Baptists, for example, found in Cromwell's New Model Army a felicitous home: members of the denomination seized the opportunity to evangelize not only within the army itself but also in the various towns and cities to which they were sent. Baptist officers in the army also organized and agitated for religious liberty until, in November 1647, the members of Parliament announced that, while everyone was required to worship on the Lord's Day, "dissenters would enjoy the liberty to meet in any fit and convenient place."[1]

For those Baptists not in the New Model Army, opportunities for evangelizing also were not lacking.

[1] William T. Shitley, *A History of British Baptists* (London: Charles Griffith, 1923), pp. 73–81.

Many leapt to fill vacancies created by priests who were declared "unfit" by the Commonwealth. In these ways Baptist congregations spread throughout England, Ireland, Scotland, and Wales.

Not everyone was pleased by this expansion, however. Other denominations felt threatened by the spread of the Baptist faith. In 1646 Presbyterian Daniel Featley wrote in his *The Dipper's Dipt* an attack upon the Baptists, saying that Baptists

> preach and print and practice their heritical impieties openly; they hold their conventicles weekly in our chief cities, and suburbs thereof. . . . They flock in great multitudes to their Jordans, and both sexes enter into the river and are dipt. . . . And as they defile our rivers with their impure washings and our pulpits with their false prophecies and fanatical enthusiasms, so the presses sweat and groan under the load of their blasphemies.

By the time of the Restoration, when the monarchy was restored to power under Charles II in 1661, the Baptists had become a major force in Britain. But spurred by protests such as Featley's, they were to endure once again a period of renewed oppression of religious dissenters. Several laws, known as the Clarendon Code, were passed to suppress nonconforming sects such as the Baptists. These laws prevented nonconformists from holding public office, attending universities, conducting services or preaching without a special license; and compelled all dissenters to attend Anglican services. Those who refused to comply with these laws were treated as anarchists and revolutionaries. They were imprisoned, tortured, and sometimes executed. John Bunyan (1628–1688) an outstanding preacher of the day who is, perhaps, best remembered for his *Pilgrim's Progress* (1678), was one who refused to obey the law forbidding preaching without a license, nor would he attend Anglican services. He was arrested in November 1660 and imprisoned for the next 12 years. However, those years were to be fruitful for Bunyan, as they provided the opportunity for study and reflection. "I never had," Bunyan wrote while in prison, "in all my life, so great an insight into the word of God as now. Those Scriptures which I saw nothing in before, are made, in this place and state, to shine upon me."

John Bunyan was released in 1672 when Charles II issued his Declaration of Indulgence which suspended the penal laws in religious matters so long as the proper licenses were obtained. The declaration was recalled in 1673 and, a few years later, Bunyan was once again imprisoned for a short time.

Similar swings between tolerance and intolerance were experienced by the Baptists during the brief reign of James II from 1685–1688. It was not until the ascension to the throne of William and Mary in 1689 and their issuance of the Act of Toleration that things stabilized. Although the Act of Toleration did not grant full religious liberty to nonconforming sects, it was a landmark in the struggle for the separation of church and state.

While the early Baptists in England, both General and Particular, were struggling for their religious freedom and identities, a similar struggle was occurring across the vast Atlantic Ocean in the new land of America to which a small number of Baptists had fled to escape the persecution in Britain. In America, as in England, the struggle for religious freedom ultimately would meet and mix with the desire for civil liberty. The result would be the birth of individual rights and—in America—the birth of a new nation.

IV

"A Lively Experiment": The Early Baptists in New England

WHILE MANY BAPTISTS WERE STRUGGLING FOR THEIR RELI-
gious liberties in England, others felt that freedom
might be better sought in the New World where dis-
tance lessened the strength of English laws. Like so
many who had made the hazardous voyage before
them, small groups of nonconforming sects fled to the
New World. Unfortunately, early settlers in the colonies

didn't find the freedom they sought to practice their faiths. Once again these nonconformists were subjected to persecution, this time from churches that already had gained a foothold in the colonies prior to their arrival. Preeminent among these groups were the Puritans.

Unlike early Calvinists who believed man was sinful but could be saved only by God's grace, the Puritans believed they had made a covenant—a bargain—with God. By promising to follow the Bible in all aspects of their lives, the Puritans would have success in this world and salvation in the next. However, man was powerless to save himself if God had predestined him to be damned. God could not be understood by man— "This sinfull creature, frail and vain. This lump of wretchness, of sin and sorrow," as man was defined by Puritan poetess Ann Bradstreet.

Because the baptism of infants "signaled membership in the covenanted community, Puritan leaders in Massachusetts were deadly serious about disciplining those who refused to comply."[1] Those sects, especially Anabaptists, practicing a "believer's" baptism (adult baptism) were singled out. In 1644 the General Court of the Massachusetts Bay Colony passed a law to deal with this refusal. The law of 1644 sought to link all who practiced believer's baptism with what the authorities felt was the heresy of the European Anabaptists "who have been the incendiaries of the commonwealth, infectors of persons and troublers of churches in all places where they have been." The

---

[1] William Henry Brackney, The Baptists (New York: Greenwood Press, 1988), p. 91.

punishment for refusal to practice infant baptism was banishment from the colony.

Similarly, membership in the Puritan church was restricted to those who could prove to the church elders

> that they are true beleevers, that they have been wounded in their hearts for the originall sinne, and actuall transgressions, and can pitch upon some promise of free grace in the Scripture, for the ground of their faith, and that they finde their hearts drawne to beleeve in Christ Jesus, for their justification and salvation . . . and that they know competently the summe of Christian faith.

Church membership was important in the Massachusetts Bay Colony, as only church members could vote and it was difficult to obtain land without it. However, although a person might be denied membership in the church, that denial did not relieve him or her of the various religious duties required and, in fact, in 1635, the Massachusetts Bay Colony had enacted a law requiring everyone to attend public worship. One who had sought freedom from these sorts of strictures in England, and who chafed under them in the New World, was Roger Williams.

Roger Williams (c. 1603–1683) is credited with having founded the first Baptist church in America—although he was a Baptist for only a short time. Born the son of a tailor in London, he was educated at Cambridge and was destined for a career in law. After graduating in 1627, however, he decided to become a minister and by 1629 had been ordained in the Anglican Church. It was undoubtedly at Cambridge that Williams first became aware of and interested in nonconformist views. After leaving Cambridge he became increasingly influenced by them. One of his early mentors was Pastor John Murton who led the first English Baptist Church after the imprisonment of Thomas Helwys.

Dissatisfied with the Church of England, Williams emigrated to Massachusetts in 1631, a staunch supporter of the separation of church and state. His arrival in the New World was anticipated by Puritan leaders with a real enthusiasm that rapidly cooled when Williams started announcing his views on the ministry, the government, and religious freedom; democratic ideas that went beyond even those of the Separatists.

After a brief period in Plymouth, Williams was sent to Salem as a minister. There he continued to express his views and in addition began to speak out for Native American rights. The royal charter, in his opinion, was merely an imperialistic expropriation of Indian rights. His congregation at Salem rejected him and he returned to Plymouth and joined the Separatist community there. In 1634 he returned to Salem as a teacher. What brought the matter of Williams's unorthodox ideas to the attention of the Massachusetts Bay Colony leaders was his denunciation of the 1635 law requiring everyone to attend public worship. The foundation of Williams's dissatisfaction was his belief in the separation of church and state. One of the four counts with which Williams was charged was his belief that "the civil magistrate's power extends only to the bodies, and goods, and outward state of men." As he was to write nine years later in The Bloudy Tenent of Persecution,

"The spiritual peace, whether true or false, is of a higher and far different nature from the peace of the place or people, which is merely and essentially civil and human."

The General Court banished Williams from the colony in 1635, and "sorely tossed for one fourteen weeks, in a bitter winter season, not knowing what bread or bed did mean," he finally made his way to Narragansett Indian country in Rhode Island. In 1636 he founded its earliest settlement at Providence—so-called, as Williams said, in remembrance of "God's merciful providence to me in my distress," as a "shelter for those distressed in conscience."

The first settlers of what was to become the Rhode Island Colony drew up a compact in which they agreed to democratic rule "only in civil things," and to allow complete freedom of worship. This covenant established Rhode Island as the first colony to guarantee full "soul liberty," as Williams called it, and the total separation of church and state.

In 1639, a few years after the founding of Providence, Williams joined the Baptist church. He liked the Baptist reliance upon Scripture and their independent attitudes. Since there was no Baptist minister in Providence, Williams followed in the footsteps of John Smyth and was baptized by Ezekiel Holliman. Holliman, along with ten others, then was baptized by Williams, thus forming the first Baptist congregation in America. After only a few months, however, Williams had rejected Baptist beliefs and become a Seeker, believing in the fundamentals of Christianity but in no creed.

Although Roger Williams left the Baptist faith, his

contribution both to the church and to America cannot be underestimated. As historian Perry Miller wrote of Williams,

> The American character has inevitably been molded by the fact that in the first years of colonization there arose this prophet of liberty. . . . As a figure and a reputation he was always there to remind Americans that no other conclusion than absolute religious freedom was feasible in this society.

Religious dissenters of all types found sanctuary in Rhode Island and the independence of the Baptist church was reaffirmed.

While Roger Williams is credited with founding the first Baptist church in America, history shows that the growth of the Baptist church in New England should be more properly credited to congregations in Newport, Swansea, and Boston.

John Clarke (1609–1676) was born on October 8, 1609, in Suffolk, England, and was trained in three professions: law, medicine, and theology. Although he had been raised in the Church of England, soon after he left school he became a Separatist and, like Williams, he sailed to the New World in search of freedom. Clarke hardly had arrived in Boston when he became embroiled in a controversy surrounding Ann Hutchinson (1591–1643), a woman whose intelligence and independence made her unique at that time. She had started weekly meetings with other women in Boston to discuss the previous Sunday's sermon, and she proposed a "covenant of grace" based on a person's direct intuition of God's grace. She was labeled an "Antino-mian" and was charged with "traducing the ministers and their ministry," and she and her family were banished from the Massachusetts Bay Colony in 1638.

In siding with Ann Hutchinson, Clarke not only fell into disfavor but also discovered for himself the intolerance prevalent in the Massachusetts Bay Colony. Chafing under the strictures of the colony, Clarke formed a company and decided to settle on the island of Aquidneck (later Newport) in Narragansett Bay. By 1648 he and his group had founded the second Baptist church in America.

Clarke, along with Obadiah Holmes and John Crandell, two other Newport Baptists, traveled to Lynn, Massachusetts, in 1651 to visit a friend, William Witter, and evangelize. When the local authorities discovered the purpose of their visit, all three men were imprisoned and fined—and Obadiah Holmes was publically whipped. Clarke wrote an account of their imprisonment, *Ill Newes From New England*, published in England in 1652. This book not only created widespread sympathy in England for the plight of the Baptists in the colonies, but later also aided Clarke's efforts, with assistance from Roger Williams, to obtain a royal charter for the Rhode Island colony—a charter that allowed for religious liberty.

In petitioning Charles II for a royal charter, Clarke wrote of Rhode Islanders that "They have it much on their hearts (if they may be permitted) to hold forth a lively experiment, that a civil state may stand . . . with a full liberty in religious concernments." The charter granted by Charles II stipulated that "noe person within the sayd colonie, at anytime hereafter shall be in any wise molested, punished, disquieted, or called in question for any differences in opinione in matters of religion." Clarke and the Baptists had triumphed, at least in Rhode Island.

While Clarke was winning tolerance for the colony of Rhode Island, similar confrontations were occurring in Massachusetts. Three years after Clarke's harassment in Lynn, Henry Dunster, the president of Harvard College, was forced to resign his position because of his negative views on infant baptism and his refusal to have his daughter baptized in the Puritan church. In 1655 the General Court of Massachusetts found Dunster guilty of disrupting a baptismal service at a Congregational church and he was forced to leave Boston.

Before he left Boston, Dunster convinced his close friend, landowner Thomas Goold, of his beliefs. Goold and others began to gather together in Goold's home and eventually formed the first Baptist congregation in Boston in 1665. His church members were denied the right to vote and frequently were fined and jailed for publicly professing their beliefs, but they persisted. Repeated imprisonment damaged Goold's health, but despite this he and his congregation erected the Boston church's first meetinghouse in 1678. The General Court immediately ordered it closed.

Although opposition to the Baptists was strong, believers in the Baptist faith surged ahead, making inroads in the stalwart and unbending Massachusetts Bay Colony. John Myles (1621–1683) was pastor to one such group. Myles was born in Wales and studied at Oxford, where it is likely he first encountered nonconformist ideas. During the years that followed Oxford, he served as a Baptist missionary in Wales. In 1663, after the passage of the Conventicle Act, Myles and his congregation decided to sail to America to avoid persecution.

After an arduous trip, Myles and his Welsh congregation first settled at Plymouth. After being fined for their beliefs by the Plymouth officials, they moved to Rehoboth (now Swansea) where, in 1663, they founded their town and church. Mindful of the persecution they had suffered, Myles and his congregation incorporated the ideas of religious freedom and charity toward others in both their town charter and church covenant. The town charter stated that "ministers of said town may take their liberty to baptize infants or grown persons as the Lord shall persuade their consciences." Similarly, their covenant noted that Christians have a "Duty to walk in visible communion with Christ and each other according to the Prescript Rule of his most Holy Word." Specifically, "The Swansea folk found it 'loathsome to their souls' to create principles or practices which divide the people of God. . . ."

Because of ideas such as those promoted by Myles and his congregation, and under pressure from King Charles II and the English Congregational ministers, the vigorous opposition to Baptists in New England lessened. In 1691, a new charter for the Massachusetts Bay Colony clearly provided for the toleration of all religious groups except Roman Catholics. Baptists also were finding, as they had in England, that it was to their benefit to have communication between their churches in order to promote the cause of religious liberty and to evangelize. The first associational meeting in America was held in 1670 among the five congregations of the General Six Principle Baptists in Rhode Island.

By 1700 the number of Baptist churches throughout New England had grown to 10, with nearly 300 members. Perhaps the most significant sign that attitudes were changing and Baptists were becoming accepted occurred in 1718 at the First Baptist Church in Boston when the Reverend Cotton Mather, that fiery defender of Puritanism, preached the ordination sermon for Elisha Callender, the first Baptist minister to be educated in America. Baptists had indeed achieved, as Roger Williams had wished, "a wider door of liberty."

V

"Agreement and Confederation"

WHILE BAPTISTS IN NEW ENGLAND WERE STRUGGLING against the unyielding wall of Puritanism, Baptists throughout the other colonies were encountering varying receptions. In the southern colonies Baptists at times encountered the same types of persecution as their brothers in New England had, this time from the Anglican Church, the dominant church in Virginia. All religious dissenters were unwelcome in Virginia, but Baptists in particular were singled out for persecution.

In 1700 a group of General Baptists holding Arminian beliefs (opposition to the idea of predestination and a belief in the salvation of all) settled in Isle of

Wight County, Virginia. In 1714 a Baptist minister, Robert Norden, arrived to organize a church at Burliegh. By midcentury, however, only a handful of churches had been founded in Berkeley, Prince George, and Loudon Counties, the majority of which embraced Calvinist doctrine.

Baptists found a warmer reception in the Carolinas, where religious toleration was granted to all dissenters in the colonies' royal charters. The first Baptists in South Carolina were from Maine. They were led by William Screven, a Maine merchant who had refused an order by Maine authorities to have his children baptized. They settled near what later was to become the port city of Charleston in 1681 and organized the first Baptist congregation in the South. The first Baptist activity in North Carolina occurred around 1714 and, in 1720, one of the first great Baptist itinerant preachers in America, Paul Palmer, arrived from Maryland. In 1727 he organized the first Baptist church in Chowan Precinct in North Carolina and in 1729 he founded another church at Shiloh in Camden County, a church still in existence today. Palmer won hundreds of converts to the Baptist faith and established churches throughout the southern and middle colonies.

Early Baptist expansion was much easier in the middle colonies of New Jersey and Pennsylvania where religious toleration was the rule. In 1684 Thomas Dungan, an Irishman who had originally settled at Newport, Rhode Island, led a group of Baptists to Cold Springs, Pennsylvania, when William Penn offered generous land grants to new settlers. The group established the first Baptist church at Cold Springs, which lasted until the end of the eighteenth century.

Four years later, in 1688, Elias Keach founded a Baptist church in Pennepack, Pennsylvania. Soon after, other congregations were established in Middletown, Cohansey, and Piscataway in New Jersey, and in Philadelphia in 1698. The Philadelphia congregation was to prove to be influential among the various Baptist churches for the next hundred years.

Many Baptists, whatever area in which they lived, were finding a need to draw together and form associations just as the General Six Principle Baptists in Rhode Island had done in 1670. Many saw the value of the sentiment expressed in the Confession of 1677, issued by the Particular Baptists of London, which stated, "Each church and all the members of it are bound to pray continually for the good and prosperity of all the churches in Christ in all places. . . . The churches ought to hold communion amongst themselves." Churches throughout the colonies were joining together, as they had in England, for mutual advice and for evangelical purposes. Most significant was the formation of the Philadelphia Association of Baptist Churches in the Delaware Valley in 1707.

Because of the religious and civil freedoms permitted in the colony of Pennsylvania, Philadelphia always had been a bustling, energetic city open to intellectual discussions and the free exchange of ideas. In the eighteenth century Philadelphia had started the first city almshouse, the first hospital, and the first penitentiary. Pennsylvania was the first colony to eliminate such punishments as the stocks and the whipping post. It is not surprising that the Philadelphia Association of Baptist Churches debated issues as diverse as the laying on of hands and membership qualifications, while other associations discussed church discipline. Five congregations from Pennsylvania, Delaware, and New Jersey made up the Philadelphia Association, agreeing to "choose particular brethren to meet yearly to consult about such things as were wanting in the churches, and to set them in order."

In keeping with the British tradition of local church autonomy, the Philadelphia Association was set up merely as an advisory organization and to promote church fellowship, although the association also assisted in raising funds for various church activities such as the education of ministers and missionary efforts. By the time of the American Revolution, the association would consist of forty churches.

In 1742 the Philadelphia Association adopted its Confession of Faith. It differed little from the Second London Confession of Faith in 1677 issued by Particular Baptists of London. In it the Philadelphia Association placed itself firmly within the Calvinist tradition, and apart from the Arminian beliefs which, until that time, had characterized the majority of Baptist congregations in America. The confession differed from the London Confession in one respect, however.

It was in the issue of the laying on of hands that the Philadelphia Association took a step away from the English Baptists. The Philadelphia Confession contained an article that read:

We believe that . . . laying on of hands (with prayer) upon baptized believers, as such, is an ordinance of Christ, and ought to be submitted unto by all such persons that are admitted to partake of the Lord's supper.

The issue of the laying on of hands had been debated by both the General and Particular Baptists since their inception and had gained acceptance among various congregations, particularly those in Wales. Many of the various churches were willing to accept the laying on of hands in connection with the ordination of elders, deacons, and ministers, but not when made a term of communion. General Baptists had accepted it as a "sixth principle" and the General Baptists in the colonies became known as the General Six Principle Baptists.

Within the individual churches making up the Philadelphia Association, some practiced the laying on of hands while others retained it only for ordination. While the article regarding the laying on of hands never was formally removed from the Philadelphia Confession, only a handful of surviving General Six Principle Baptist churches in New England and a few General Baptist churches in the southern states retain it as a requirement for new members.

In 1746 the Philadelphia Association felt that a history of the association should be written and, in 1749, Benjamin Griffith, pastor of the Montgomery, Pennsylvania, church, produced an essay "which became the classic statement of the purpose of Baptist Associations in America."[1] Reinforcing the basic ideas of autonomy and voluntary membership, Griffith wrote, "an Association is not a superior judicature, having such superior power over the churches concerned . . . ," rather the individual churches "may, and ought, . . . by their vol-

---

[1] William Henry Brackney, *The Baptists* (New York: Greenwood Press, 1988), p. 74.

untary and free consent, to enter into an agreement and confederation."

With the principles of associations formally delineated in Griffith's essay, association sprang up among the individual churches of the colonies like weeds. Between 1775 and 1815, 104 new associations were created. However, although regional associations flourished, any attempts at centralization were resisted stoutly. Most associational leaders felt that all associations should be equal and that centralization under one organization would mean some loss of independence. They also felt that there was no need for centralization.

By the mid-eighteenth century the genesis of the Baptist organizational structure had been completed. Although individually many of the Baptist churches were struggling still for freedom within their separate colonies, they were strong and independent within their own associations and a network of communication had been established. This network was to strengthen and grow to create, in the twentieth century, one of the strongest organizational structures extant among religions today.

VI

The Great Awakening

FOR MANY OF THE FIRST SETTLERS TO ARRIVE ON AMER-
ica's shores, their deep religious convictions helped
them overcome the many hardships to be faced in tam-
ing the harsh, new wilderness. But, as time went on
and conditions began to improve, interest in religion
began to wane in the colonies to such an extent that by
the start of the eighteenth century there was an actual
decline in church membership.

The reasons behind the decline in religious activities
are varied. As the colonies began to produce greater
wealth, people became more interested in material
rather than spiritual pursuits. Political issues also at-

tracted more attention, as did recurring wars, particularly with Indians on the western frontier. At the same time the dominant churches were growing lax in their attention to pastoral duties. Fewer men felt the call to the ministry. With a lack of preachers to inspire them, people naturally turned away from the churches.

In America people were exploring the ideas sweeping Europe and England during this so-called Age of Enlightenment. Toward the end of the seventeenth century, a "rational theology" emerged in England that was taken up by a large and influencial group called Latitudinarians. The members of this group included some very influencial men, among whom was John Tillotson, Archbishop of Canterbury from 1691 to 1694. Tillotson and the Latitudinarians advocated using reason in reading the Scriptures and denounced the emotional transports encouraged by revivalist religions. The Latitudinarian ideas were adopted and expanded upon by philosopher John Locke in his *Reasonableness of Christianity*. Although Locke believed that Jesus Christ was the Messiah, much of Christianity, he felt, could be explained either rationally or as being the invention of superstitious or power-hungry priests.

From Locke it was but a short step to Deism, the belief that the only proof of God's existence lay in his visible works. Deists believed that God, having created the world and the universe and set them in motion, then abandoned them. Having abandoned the universe, God assumed no control over a person's life, set no guidelines, and exerted no influence. An individual was left alone to direct his or her own life.

Deism was popular with many people during the eighteenth century, partly because it relieved them of any obligations toward established religions. In England it served the political interests in undercutting the influence of the established religions on the state.

In Europe a similar loosening of the religious reins was occurring. The austere teachings of Calvinism were losing their fervor. Ministers, like their Latitudinarian counterparts in England, were preaching the virtues of reason and the innate goodness of man. Such ideas could not but help filter across the Atlantic to the New World, and many people found these ideas agreeable. Benjamin Franklin was himself a Deist but felt that uneducated, "humble" people had "need of the motives of religion to restrain them from vice, to support their virtue, and retain them in practice of it till it become habitual. . . ."

Just when this spiritual ebb seemed to have reached its lowest point, a religious revival swept the American colonies. The Great Awakening, as it was called, was sparked during the 1720s by two ministers from New Jersey: Theodore Frelinghuysen, a Dutch Reformed evangelist; and Gilbert Tennent, a Presbyterian. Puritan theologian Jonathan Edwards brought the revival to New England in the 1730s. Edwards is perhaps the best-remembered leader of the Great Awakening because his sermons thrilled his listeners and filled them with the fear of hell-fire and damnation:

> The God that holds you over the pit of hell, much as one holds a spider or some loathsome insect over the fire, abhors you, and is dreadfully provoked. You are ten thousand times so abominable in his eyes, as the most hateful and venomous serpent. . . . If you cry to God to pity you, He will

be so far from pitying you in your doleful case, or showing you the least regard or favor, that instead of that, He will only tread you under foot.

Edwards brought about numerous conversions and was followed and often imitated by other evangelizing ministers. Among these was George Whitefield, the English evangelist, who inspired the spiritual reawakening of literally thousands of Americans.

George Whitefield's message was similar to Edwards's, but his delivery was much more dramatic; so much so that his Anglican superiors in England had removed him from the pulpit for his "ranting and raving." Contemporary accounts note that he was cross-eyed, which probably only added to the dramatic effect. After one of his sermons, "some were struck pale as Death, others wringing their hands, others lying on the ground, others sinking into the arms of their friends, and most lifting up their eyes toward heaven, and crying out to GOD." Although Whitefield was an Anglican with Calvinist convictions, thousands of people from all denominations throughout the colonies flocked to his great outdoor services to hear him preach. In Philadelphia, for example, Whitefield spoke from the Gallery of the Court House to a crowd of 6,000 people standing in the streets below.

Because of its broad democratic appeal, the Great Awakening marked the dawn of a new era of growth among dissenting denominations in America. The Great Awakening so popularized evangelical Christianity that it became socially acceptable, even fashionable, to withdraw from the established churches to join evangelical sects such as the Baptists. These so-called

"Separates" or "New Light" Baptists were mildly Calvinistic in their beliefs and occasionally practiced infant baptism. Because of this they often encountered conflict with other, "Old Light" Baptists.

The Separates of the Great Awakening took their name from a sect already established in the colonies at the time. The Separates had arrived in the colonies in 1695 as one group fleeing persecution in England and were an offshoot of the Separatist movement there. With the Great Awakening, the Separates seized the opportunity to increase their membership. The Separates demanded a tightening-up of what they felt was the moral laxity of the time. They criticized the effectiveness of the established churches and of lay authorities to create a moral society. So fervent were they that, in 1743, the Toleration Act was revoked in Connecticut. "Itinerant evangelists were billed as troublemakers and the Separate meetings were called illegal conventicles."[1]

In 1787 Separate and Regular Baptist churches merged in Virginia to create the United Baptist Churches of Christ in Virginia. There were other mergers between New Light and Old Light churches, but a few Separate churches maintain their independence even today with their own churches, associations, and missionary programs.

As New England Baptists began to catch the revival fever, the result was a strengthening of already established churches and the founding of splinter groups for those who did not agree with the views of the estab-

[1] William Henry Brackney, *The Baptists* (New York: Greenwood Press, 1988), p. 96.

lished churches. The schism among the Baptists resulted in the creation of a number of new Baptist groups, although one of the earliest had begun in England in the mid-seventeenth century, the Seventh-Day Baptists.

The Seventh-Day Baptists, as their name attests, felt that the Bible dictated that the Sabbath fall on the seventh day (Saturday) rather than Sunday. The first established Seventh-Day Baptist church in America began in 1671 at Newport, Rhode Island, under the leadership of Stephen Mumford, a Sabbatarian from London. By 1790 Seventh-Day Baptists had grown to comprise seven groups in New England and New York.

The Rhode Island group was completely separate from yet another Sabbatarian group, the Seventh-Day Baptist (German) group established in 1728 by John Conrad Beissel, a Palatinate German, in Germantown, Pennyslvania. The German Sabbatarians gained few converts because of their monastic requirements. In 1732 they established a community at Ephrata, Pennsylvania, in which all goods were held in common and men and women lived in separate houses under a rule requiring celibacy. By the mid-twentieth century, the church reportedly had only 150 members in three churches.

One splinter group of Baptists that had moderate success was the Free Will Baptist Connection. The Free Will Baptists in America originated in Wales and came to the New World in 1701, settling in Pennsylvania. They experienced some success in their evangelical efforts; in 1727 the Free Will Baptists were organized in the South by Paul Palmer. They gained more converts, however, in the North under the leadership of Benjamin Randall (1749–1808).

During the 1770s, 21-year-old Benjamin Randall heard George Whitefield preach. After being roused by Whitefield's eloquence, Randall returned to his church, the New Castle Congregational Church in New Castle, New Hampshire, but he soon was disillusioned by what he felt was the church's lack of fervor. With the birth of his third child and after studying his Bible, Randall concluded that he couldn't baptize his child in the Congregationalist faith. He concluded that infant baptism was not scriptural and that he himself should seek immersion as a believer. Randall was baptized in 1776, joined the Baptist movement, and began a career in preaching. In 1778 he assumed the pastorship of a Baptist church in New Durham, New Hampshire, but his preaching soon led to dissension. He stressed the idea of universal atonement and emphasized "free grace, free will, and free communion," In 1779 Randall was called to explain his views in a debate with Regular Baptists at Gilmanton. During the debate he repudiated much of the Calvinistic doctrine. As a result, mainstream Baptists disowned him. Randall organized a small group from his congregation who shared his beliefs into the Free Will Baptist Connection on June 30, 1780, forming a covenant "according to Scripture and necessary for the visible government of the Church of Christ." Randall was an enthusiastic organizer and evangelist. He set up a Free Will organization based on the Quaker system of meetings and traveled extensively throughout New Hampshire and Maine. Within three years he had started fourteen churches.

The Great Awakening also brought about the establishment of black Baptist churches. As early as 1700, many white slaveholders in the South were providing religious instruction to their slaves. However, black slaves were forced to sit in a separate section of the white churches or not permitted to attend services at all. Many colonies passed laws forbidding the establishment of black churches. Despite these obstacles, and under the influence of the fervor generated by the Great Awakening, black churches grew in both the North and the South. The first black Baptist church in America was organized at Silver Bluff across the Savannah River from Augusta, Georgia, in 1773. Other churches quickly followed in Petersburg, Virginia, in 1776; Richmond, Virginia, in 1780; Williamsburg, Virginia, in 1785; Savannah, Georgia, in 1785, and Lexington, Kentucky, in 1790. Similar churches were founded in New York and Philadelphia in the early 1800s.

Like many other Christian groups, white Baptists were not prepared for racial integration. Hence, black Baptists for the most part were forced to seek fellowship and help among themselves. The first black association was created in Ohio in 1834 for that purpose. The black Baptist churches have flourished and grown since the Great Awakening. By the middle of the twentieth century, nearly 50 percent of all American blacks belonged to the Baptist faith.

Two other groups having their roots in the religious enthusiasm of the eighteenth century, but only finally emerging in the nineteenth century, deserve mention: the Two-Seed-in-the-Spirit Predestination Baptists and the Primitive Baptists, both of whom are strictly orthodox.

The Two-Seed-in-the-Spirit Predestination Baptists

emerged in the early nineteenth century out of the protests of Elder Daniel Parker (1781–1844) of Virginia. Parker had been protesting against the Arminian doctrine and against the missionary efforts of the church and church schools. He used as his rationale what he called his "Two-Seed Doctrine" based on Genesis 3:15. He felt that the Bible indicated that two seeds entered the world in the Garden of Eden. One seed was good, planted by God; the other seed was evil, planted by Satan. Every baby is predestined, according to Parker's belief, to good or evil, being born of one seed or the other. Human history thus becomes the struggle between the two sides until Satan finally is defeated by God. With the stress on God's wisdom and power, Parker saw no reason to teach or do missionary work. Parker was described as "at once uncouth, slovenly, pugnacious, eloquent, perceptive and forceful."[2] The Two-Seed-in-the-Spirit Predestination Baptist churches had only a loose organizational structure. As the years have passed, they have lost membership, with only a few churches remaining today.

The Primitive Baptists, unlike the Two-Seed-in-the-Spirit Predestination Baptists, have grown in membership since their inception. The Primitive Baptists are perhaps the most strictly orthodox and exclusive of all Baptists. The Primitive Baptists grew out of a protest against "money-based" missions and against "assessing" the churches to support missions and missionaries in the early nineteenth century. The Primitive Baptists are strictly Calvinistic in their orientation and

[2] *Ibid.*, p. 241.

membership is granted only after a careful examination and vote by the congregation. By the mid-twentieth century, they were estimated to have a membership of approximately 70,000 in 1,000 churches, although factionalism, politics, and divisiveness have prevented an accurate count of their membership.

By the end of the eighteenth century, the Baptist denomination was growing and spreading, largely due to the Great Awakening and the zealous evangelical efforts of the Baptists themselves. Hezekiah Smith (1737–1805), a great itinerant evangelist of the day, helped found 86 new Baptist churches in Massachusetts alone, and preached as far north as the frontiers of Maine. Prior to the Great Awakening, there were five Baptist churches in Massachusetts. By the end of the century that number had risen to over 135. In 1740 there were two Baptist churches in Connecticut; in 1800 there were 60. In Rhode Island the number rose from 11 to 40 during the same period, and the first Baptist college—the third college of any kind in New England—was founded in Warren in 1764. The College of Rhode Island, established to train much-needed ministers to serve the growing denomination, was dedicated to the idea of full religious liberty. In 1770 the college was moved to Providence and later renamed Brown University.

In Vermont and New Hampshire some 40 Baptist societies had been established by 1800 where before there had been none. Overall, the total number of Baptist congregations in New England had risen to 325 by 1800 and a similar surge of Baptist growth was to be seen throughout the young country. Such rapid growth did not go unopposed by the established churches, but there seemed little they could do to stem the tide that would, one day, make the Baptist church the number one Protestant denomination in the United States.

VII

"Liberty and Toleration"

FOR A MAJORITY OF SETTLERS IN AMERICA, THE AMERICAN revolution was more than just a protest against "taxation without representation." The "shot heard round the world," fired on April 19, 1775, heralded the desire on the colonists' part for freedom in all aspects of their lives. For the various Baptist sects at the time it manifested itself in the desire for complete religious liberty and a freedom from persecution.

For Baptists the original enemy was not the British per se but the Congregational and Anglican church establishments. In Virginia, where the Anglican church was closely identified with the English overlord, the

Baptist struggle for religious freedom and the patriots' cause were united, and many Baptists served in the vanguard of the army.

In New England, where the Congregationalists tended to support the Revolution, the situation was a bit different for Baptists. But when Baptists began to be hounded and tormented by the British—in 1776, for example, British troops burned a Baptist meetinghouse in Rhode Island and took the minister captive—Baptists put aside their animosity toward the established church and fought side by side with Congregationalists against the common enemy. Isaac Backus (1724–1806) noted that the Baptists in Massachusetts were so wholeheartedly behind the revolution that when the General Court of Boston published a list of 311 men who were considered enemies of the state because of their sympathy with the British, not one Baptist appeared on the list.

Isaac Backus had been a longtime champion of religious liberty and became even more fervent after his own widowed mother was jailed by the Puritans in 1752 for refusing to pay the ministerial tax and for her pietistic devotion to what she felt to be the will of God. Backus is representative of the influence of the Great Awakening. In his late teens, he heard itinerant evangelists Eleazer Wheelock, James Pomeroy, and George Whitefield preach in his hometown of Norwich, Connecticut. With his mother and others, Backus left his church, the Norwich Congregational Church, in 1744. He soon joined with a group of Separates in Titicut, Massachusetts, and consented to become their pastor in 1748. The church often hosted itinerant Baptist preachers, and through them Backus became aware of the issue of infant baptism. Finally, after much study, Backus was baptized in 1751 and within five years had organized the Baptist congregation he would serve for the next 50 years.

As the enthusiasm and fervor of the Great Awakening declined, there was again an increase of persecution against dissenting sects in the colonies. Noah Worcester, a devout Congregationalist, later summed up the feelings of many of his contemporaries about Baptists in his scathing attack entitled *Impartial Inquiries, Respecting the Progress of the Baptist Denomination*, published in 1794:

> Many people are so ignorant as to be charmed with sound rather than sense. And to them, the want of knowledge in a teacher . . . may easily be made up, and overbalanced by great zeal, an affecting tone of voice, and a perpetual motion of tongue. If a speaker can keep his tongue running in an unremitting manner . . . and can quote from memory a large number of texts from within the covers of the Bible, it matters not to his hearers whether he speaks *sense* or *nonsense*.

When attitudes such as this became increasingly prevalent, religious liberty became even more threatened, and the problem of unfair taxation was added. Isaac Backus, always a dynamic leader, joined with other ministers to organize the Warren Baptist Association in 1767 (although his own church didn't join until 1770, fearing a loss of their autonomy). The Warren Baptist Association was formed for the purpose of spearheading the struggle for religious freedom. Backus served as the agent of the Warren Baptist Association many times and, in his extensive travels on their behalf, was strident in voicing both his and the association's demands for religious freedom.

By establishing a connection between Baptist principles and the emerging democratic feeling among Americans, Backus broadened the base of Baptist appeal and helped Baptists win wider acceptance and a new aura of respectability in the colonies. In his *Appeal to the Public for Religious Liberty Against the Oppression of the Present Day*, written on the eve of the American Revolution in 1773, Backus pointed out that the patriots' demand to England for "No taxation without representation" was meaningless if they, in turn, required those who did not belong to the established churches to pay taxes for their support. In 1774, he wrote,

We Baptists are determined not to pay taxes for church support not only upon the patriots' principle of not being taxed where we are not represented, but also because we dare not render that homage to any earthly power which I and my brethren are fully convinced belongs only to God.

While Backus acknowledged the importance of the "general union" of the colonies for the "preservation of liberties," he asked, "How can such a union be expected so long as that dearest of all rights, equal liberty of conscience, is not allowed?"

Because of his eloquence and enthusiasm, Backus was sent in 1774 as an agent to plead the case for religious liberty to the Continental Congress. In their petition Backus and the Warren Baptist Association wrote, "We claim and expect the liberty of worshipping God according to our consciences, not being obliged to support a ministry we cannot attend."

While Backus was there, he also met with delegates from Massachusetts, New Jersey, and Pennsylvania and urged them to support the disestablishment of the Congregational church in Massachusetts, although with little luck. John Adams is reported to have remarked, "The Baptists might as well expect a change in the solar system as to expect that the Massachusetts authorities would give up their establishment."

Americans were waging a war on two fronts: "While the defense of the civil rights of America appeared a matter of great importance," Backus was later to write, "our religious liberties were by no means to be neglected; and the contest concerning each kept a pretty even pace throughout the war."

In the southern colonies a similar struggle was occurring. For years Baptists had sought to loosen the stranglehold the Anglican church had on the colony of Virginia, for example. By the start of the American Revolution, the number of religious dissenters in Virginia totaled more than half the population, and these, along with the many Anglicans who were appalled at the growing corruption within their own church, now were ready to support the cause of religious freedom.

John Leland (1754–1841) was to the South what Isaac Backus had been to New England and the North. Leland was self-taught and known to his acquaintances to be shrewd, witty, and eccentric. In 1772, at the age of 18, he was converted after hearing Elhanan Winchester, an itinerant preacher, speak in Massachusetts. After being ordained as a minister, he and his young wife moved to Virginia around 1776. He traveled as an evangelist and served as pastor of the Mount Poney Baptist Church in Culpepper, Virginia, until 1792, when he returned to Massachusetts.

Leland is said to have influenced the thought of James Madison and Thomas Jefferson on the matter of religious liberty. Leland was an outspoken opponent of state-supported churches or, as he put it, religion that is "a principle of state" rather than true "Bible religion." According to Leland

> Government should protect every man in thinking and speaking freely and see that one does not abuse another. The liberty that I contend for is more than toleration. The very idea of toleration is despicable; it supposes that some have a preeminence above the rest to grant indulgence; whereas all should be equally free, Jews, Turks, pagans and Christians. Test oaths and established creeds should be avoided as the worst of evils.

Leland worked locally for the cause of religious freedom, but his influence was felt throughout the colonies. Fearing the centralization of authority, whether civil or religious, Leland opposed the idea of a constitutional convention when he heard one was proposed. In a letter, Leland listed ten reasons for his opposition, the final being: "It is very dangerous to leave religious liberty at the mercy of people whose manners are corrupted." According to legend, the opposition Leland expressed affected at least one signer of the Constitution.

As the story goes, John Leland planned to run for election as a delegate to the Virginia Convention called to ratify the Constitution. He intended to petition the convention to change the Constitution to include a more definite guarantee of religious freedom. He was a popular and well-known figure in Virginia and was sure to win a seat at the convention, but before the election, Leland is reported to have met with James Madison at a location in what is now known as Leland-Madison State Park. At that meeting, Leland agreed to withdraw from the race in favor of Madison because he believed Madison had more political influence in the new federal government. In exchange for Leland's promise to withdraw from the election, Madison pledged to introduce an amendment to the Constitution that would guarantee the separation of church and state in America.

Madison was elected to the convention, where he helped compose the first amendment of the Bill of Rights to the Constitution, adopted in 1789. It states, "Congress shall make no law respecting an establishment of religion, or prohibiting the free exercise thereof." Although it did not extend as far as John Leland wished, this amendment represents a landmark in the history of church-state relations.

On the national level, the struggle for religious liberty was victorious due to the efforts of men like Isaac Backus and John Leland, and during the Revolution and after, similar victories were won within the various states. In 1776, for example, the Baptists petitioned the Virginia House of Burgesses for complete religious liberty. In June of that year, the House passed a Declaration of Rights that allowed for the freedom to practice any religion. It did not end the influence of the Anglican Church, however. Over the following years, a number of petitions and bills were presented that called for the end of the church establishment. One was introduced in 1779 by Thomas Jefferson. In 1783, however, Regular and Separate Baptists joined forces in a Baptist General Committee to press the cause for religious liberty in Virginia. They worked closely with Presbyterians, Catholics, and Quakers, and it was largely due to their efforts that Jefferson's bill finally was passed by the legislature in 1785. The bill became a model for similar legislation throughout the South, where Anglicanism soon was completely disestablished.

It took a while before church disestablishment became a reality in New England. The Congregationalists had been staunch supporters of the revolution. They were not identified with Britain as were the Anglicans, and many had taken a hand in the forming of the new nation. They were anxious to maintain their position of religious and political supremacy after the war had ended.

In Connecticut, where the Congregationalists still dominated the civil government after the war, one-third of the population was made up of dissenters. Baptists were in the forefront of the movement to topple the Congregationalist establishment, and it was largely due to their agitation that the Toleration Act became law in 1784. The act allowed residents of the state to pay taxes to support the churches of their choice. This legislation was not considered far-reaching enough by most Baptists, who continued to suffer persecution—having their property confiscated, being imprisoned, and so forth—at the hands of civil authorities well into the nineteenth century. Baptists finally prevailed, however, at the Connecticut Constitutional Convention in 1818, where legislation was passed to put an end to the church establishment in Connecticut.

In 1817 the Congregationalist establishment was brought down in New Hampshire. It wasn't until 1833, however, that the last vestiges of the established church were wiped out in that traditional Congregational stronghold, Massachusetts.

After nearly 200 years of ceaseless agitation, Baptists finally achieved their goal of complete religious liberty in the new American nation. Without constantly having to struggle against oppressive local and state laws, Baptists now were free to "promote the knowledge of evangelical truth" throughout the United States and, ultimately, the world. The fierce independence that had characterized the Baptists since their inception had found a home in the nation that was soon to become known, because of the independence of its people, as the "land of the free."

VIII

"A Heavenly Confusion": The Great Revival

BAPTISTS, LIKE OTHER EVANGELICAL PROTESTANT DE-
nominations, experienced a decline in membership
during the war years. The focus was on the battle for
independence, not on the hereafter. In addition, the
British destroyed many Baptist churches and imprisoned many Baptist ministers; there was little time
or opportunity to evangelize in the midst of battle. Yet
evangelizing is basic to most Baptists; most feel that
every Christian is an evangelist and is committed to

proclaiming the Christian faith and trying to win others to it.

After the war was over and the church establishment was destroyed in most states, Baptists were at last able to concentrate on winning new converts without hindrance, and the growth of the denomination during the 30 years following the end of the Revolutionary War was both rapid and unprecedented. This was spurred, in part, by the organization of the Baptist Missionary Society in 1792 in Britain, which stimulated the formation of similar missionary groups in America.

First known as the English Particular Baptist Society for the Propagation of the Gospel Among the Heathen, the Baptist Missionary Society was organized by William Carey (1761–1834) in Kettering, England. Carey urged all Christians, but especially the Baptists, to go forth and convert the heathen. His words were simple: "Pray, plan, pay," and they "breathed new life into a fragmented and sagging Baptist body" in England.[1] In the new United States, the focus upon evangelical efforts provided a sense of unity and purpose to postwar Baptists.

By the opening of the nineteenth century, the Baptist denomination in the United States was no longer the despised, outcast sect it once had been, but now was a prominent part of the American religious mainstream. It had become, without question, the favored religion of the new American nation, reflecting as it did the ideals of liberty and democracy the patriots had fought for

[1] William Henry Brackney, *The Baptists* (New York: Greenwood Press, 1988), p. 14.

and had died to preserve. Yet, though favored among religions, religion itself was out of favor.

The same liberty that the Baptist denomination enjoyed—the freedom to do as one wished—had had a disquieting effect on the young country after the war. The pursuit of money and success was pushing aside the more down-to-earth virtues, and religion seemed to be dying under the wheels of progress and change. Faced with a decline in religion occasioned by the myriad opportunities offered in America, by the flood of immigrants surging to the shores of the new country, and by the sudden changes in technology, the clergy resorted to the vigorous and emotional counter-offensive known as the Great Revival or the Second Great Awakening.

The Great Revival began in colleges in the 1780s and had two phases. The first phase was characterized by an orderly renewal of religious commitment in the older, more conservative churches of the East. The second phase, which took place on the western frontier, was much more emotional in nature. People flocked to hear the harangues of revivalist preachers at the great outdoor camp meetings that sometimes lasted for days. These revivals peaked around the middle of the nineteenth century but have continued to be popular on and off to this day.

The theology of the revivalists reflected the new American democratic spirit. Turning away from the strict Calvinism preached in the revivals of the First Great Awakening, the evangelists of the Great Revival tended to emphasize good works as a means to salvation. The Baptists, like the other Protestant religions, used the Great Revival as a most effective evangelical tool, and the gains they made were even more impressive that those of the First Great Awakening. From Maine to Georgia, Baptist preachers tirelessly spread the word, gathering thousands of converts to the fold. In Virginia, Baptists soon outstripped all other denominations in membership, and by 1800, the Baptist denomination had become the fastest-growing religious movement in America.

Baptists made their greatest gains along the rough, lonely western frontier. As the American nation expanded westward, the Baptist denomination grew right along with it. Whole congregations joined the westward migration, fleeing economic depression in the Northeast and continued Anglican persecution in the South. The "traveling churches," as they were called, were made up of small farmers and their families who settled the fertile regions west of the Allegheny Mountains and south of the Ohio River. They were welcomed in the bare outreaches where there was no established church and where going to church was the social event of the week. Similarly, the camp meetings provided not only spiritual uplift but entertainment for lonely frontier families; they were an occasion to see others from the area, exchange news, and if so moved, save one's soul.

The revivals of the Great Revival were a great boon to Baptist growth on the frontier as well as providing entertainment. Robert Sample characterized the Baptist revivals of the era in his *A History of the Rise and Progress of the Baptists in Virginia*, published in 1810:

It was not unusual to have a large proportion of a congregation prostrate on the floor; and, in some instances they have lost the use of their limbs. No distinct articulation could be heard unless from those immediately by. Screams, cries, groans, songs, shouts and hosannas, notes of grief and notes of joy, all heard at the same time, made a heavenly confusion, a sort of indescribable concert. Even the wicked and unenlightened were astonished and said, the Lord hath done great things for his people. At Associations and great meetings, where there were several ministers, many of them would exercise their gifts at the same time in different parts of the congregation; some in exhortation; some in praying for the distressed; and some in argument with opposers. At first many of the preachers did not approve of this kind of work. They thought it extravagant. Others found it fire from heaven. It is not unworthy of notice that in those congregations where the preachers encouraged these exercises to much extent the work was more extensive and greater numbers were added.

By the mid-1780s there were enough Baptist churches on the frontier to form associations. The Elkhorn Association, formed by representatives of six Regular Baptist churches in Kentucky in September 1785, was the first Baptist organization west of the Alleghenies. In October of that same year, another association was founded by Regular Baptists farther west in Salem, Kentucky.

In 1787, Separate Baptists organized the Southern Kentucky Association. In 1800, the Elkhorn and Southern Kentucky Associations united. This union of Separate and Regular Baptists reflected the frontier Baptists' preference for a compromise between Regular (Calvinistic) and Separate (Arminian) doctrine that resulted in a more liberal, less severe Calvinism. In Tennessee the Holston Association, formed in 1786, contained both Regular and Separate Baptists.

By 1810 there were 15 Baptist associations in Kentucky representing 286 churches with 16,650 members. In Tennessee there were six associations with 102 churches and 11,693 members. The frontier was welcoming the Baptist denomination with open arms.

The preacher was the heart and soul of the Baptist revival on the frontier. He generally came from the same common pioneer stock as the members of his congregation; most Baptist preachers were farmers themselves who worked right alongside their flocks, clearing the land, planting crops, and raising cows and chickens. What these farmer-preachers lacked in formal education, they more than made up for in dedication and inspiration. Since they had no financial or political ties to any ecclesiastical organization, they were free to travel about the widely scattered pioneer settlements gathering new congregations wherever they went. Some congregations consisted of only a handful of believers, and church buildings generally were simple wood structures named for a nearby creek, river, or valley.

The pioneers were hungry for spiritual sustenance and the Baptist farmer-preacher carried it to them in a form they easily could digest. He spoke the same language as the pioneers and understood their problems because he shared them, unlike the university-trained and aloof ministers of the established churches. The simplicity of the Baptist doctrine and the democracy of their church organization were more to the pioneers' liking. In short, the Baptist denomination found on the American frontier an atmosphere particularly congenial to its message and style.

John Taylor was an outstanding representative of the Baptist farmer-preacher of the day. An Anglican born in Virginia, he was "awakened" at the age of 17 and later converted to the Baptist faith. After he was ordained a preacher, he migrated to Kentucky with his pregnant wife and served as pastor of the Clear Creek Church. He preached all across the frontier, helping to establish approximately 70 Baptist churches in western Virginia, North Carolina, Tennessee, and Kentucky. In addition to his pastoral work, Taylor managed to raise a large family, clear and farm over 400 acres of land, amass a large fortune, and in 1823 publish his valuable first-hand account of early Baptist activity on the frontier, *History of Ten Baptist Churches*.

Baptists were not alone, of course, in their sponsorship of frontier revivals and in frontier evangelizing. Other Protestant denominations, particularly the Methodists, also were engaged actively in evangelizing among the pioneers. Interdenominational cooperation was the hallmark of the Great Revival, and preachers from different denominations often shared the same revival platforms, although a kind of friendly rivalry grew up among the various groups. This competition is reflected in a popular Methodist song of the day and the Baptist response to it. The subject is the Baptist practice of baptism by immersion. The Methodists sang:

> We've searched the law of heaven
> Throughout the sacred code;
> Of Baptism there by dipping

We've never found a word.

To plunge is inconsistent
Compared with holy rites;
An instance of such business
We've never found as yet.

To which the Baptists replied:

Not *at* the River Jordan
But *in* its flowing stream
Stood John the Baptist preacher
When he baptized Him.

John was a Baptist preacher
When he baptis'd the Lamb;
Then Jesus was a Baptist
And thus the Baptists came.

Although there was rivalry, that rivalry was for the most part friendly. Most at the time felt there was room enough and sinners enough in this great, wide, new land for all.

In addition to ministering to the spiritual needs of the pioneers, the churches also often acted as the final moral authority on the frontier. There were very few formal controls on behavior in the sparsely settled territories of the West. There were no police, no sheriff or courts of law, and, as a consequence, frontier justice was a pretty rough, disorganized, and localized affair. Most frontiersmen craved some order in the midst of the moral chaos that often characterized much of frontier life, and although church membership in any frontier settlement represented a relatively small part of the total population, the majority of the settlers tended to look to the local church to set the moral tone and rules of conduct for the entire community and to discipline those who strayed from those high standards. Monthly church business meetings often were given over to the business of administering discipline, and Baptist church records of the day often read like a catalog of misdemeanors and disciplinary actions. Drunkenness, fighting, stealing, and adultery were the most common problems the church had to confront. Other conduct that commonly merited punishment included mistreatment of a wife or a slave, absence from church meetings, swearing, "superfluity" in dress, horse racing, gambling, "and in brief, all those exercises and entertainments of pastime and merriment commonly termed recreations." Punishment for misconduct ranged from public censure to excommunication from the congregation.

By the beginning of the nineteenth century, the Baptist denomination had become one of the leading and fastest-growing Protestant denominations in America. Although Baptist strength still lay largely with the common man, the denomination now could count among its members many people of wealth and influence who contributed to the denomination's growing respectability.

A number of factors contributed to this Baptist expansion. In addition to the upsurge in revivalism was the fact that the Baptist church was one of the most indigenously American of all denominations, having grown up with and contributed to the political development of the new nation. Baptists were helped by the freedom of their preachers and evangelists. Baptist ministers were free agents, and many dedicated farmer-preachers were able to carry the Gospel to the frontier. They also were helped in their endeavors by the Baptist doctrine, which was simple enough for all men to grasp. Finally, the denomination's democratic organization appealed to Americans, particularly the pioneers who so greatly prized individuality and independence and who had taken up the challenge of the wilderness to escape the more structured confines of the city with its rules and crowding.

The seeds sown by the preachers of the Great Revival already were bearing fruit in the nineteenth century in newly formed missionary and Sunday school movements, the founding of church-affiliated colleges and universities, and the establishment of philanthropic and humanitarian institutions. The "heavenly confusion" of the Great Revival was giving way to an earthly organization.

IX

"Spreading Evangelical Truth": The Baptist Missionary Movement

IN THE MID-1830S DIARIST PHILIP HONE'S WRITINGS RE-flected the concerns many Americans felt about their country. "There is an awful tendency toward insubor-dination and contempt of the laws," he lamented, "and there is reason to apprehend that good order and morality will ere long be overcome by intemperance and violence . . . . My poor country, what is to be the issue of the violence of the people . . .?" In the cities in particular, vice seemed rampant. A growing population meant an increased poor population; prostitution, drunkenness, and other more criminal activities were on the rise. One "issue" of all this was a growth in the missionary efforts of various denominations, particularly the Baptists.

Historically, Baptists always have felt that every church member is an evangelist and has a duty to spread the ideas of Christianity and the acceptance of those ideas among others. Evangelizing had been the duty of every church member, but, in America it had not been under the guidance of any formal organization until the 1800s. In 1800 interest was expressed in a more organized evangelical effort when Mary Webb (1779–1861), a member of Boston's Second Baptist Church, formed the first voluntary society among American Baptists, The Boston Female Society for Missionary Purpose. Crippled from the age of five, Webb nonetheless managed to organize and run the society from her home. Initially, Webb only raised money for William Carey's British Baptist Missionary Society but later, in 1816, she established a mission for the poor in Boston and undertook evangelical work among prostitutes. Her example, combined with the vision and efforts of her minister, Thomas Baldwin (1753–1825), led to the creation of the Massachusetts Baptist Missionary Society in 1802. Its purpose was "to furnish occasional preaching and to promote the knowledge of evangelical truth in new settlements within these

United States or farther if circumstances should render it proper."

The Massachusetts Baptist Missionary Society was but one response to the seeming decadence of the nineteenth century and to the growing recognition among Baptists that there was a need for a more organized evangelical effort on the expanding frontier. The western territories were too vast for the old-time farmer-preacher or itinerant minister to handle on his own. Spurred by the examples of the Baptist Missionary Society in Britain and the Massachusetts Baptist Missionary Society, voluntary groups and societies sprang up everywhere with one intent being to take the Word to the "Godless" frontiers of the young United States.

The missionary's life was not an easy one. Traveling on horseback or often by foot, he had to cross mountains and ford rivers in all seasons and weather. It was not unusual for a missionary to cover 5,000 miles of uncharted territory in a single year. The missionary, traveling and living in a tent or covered wagon, ministering to the small settlements that could not support a church, was a distinctive feature of the Great Plains.

One of the most outstanding Baptist missionaries and leaders of the early frontier missionary effort was John Mason Peck (1789–1858). Born in Connecticut and self-taught, Peck was converted at the age of 18 and ordained a minister at 25. In 1815 he met Luther Rice, who had helped organize the first General Mission Convention of the Baptist denomination the previous year. Rice urged Peck to join the missionary movement and, although he suffered from poor health, he decided to brave the many hardships of frontier life in order to carry the Gospel to the West. Peck was sent to St. Louis to form "Regular" Baptist churches and evangelize among the Indians. After a journey of 128 days in a one-horse wagon, he arrived in St. Louis and established the first Baptist church in the Missouri Territory. Peck went on to establish 50 public schools, as well as numerous Bible societies and Sunday schools throughout the Illinois and Missouri regions. His publications, *Guide to Emigrants* (1831) and *Gazetteer of Illinois* (1836), attracted many new settlers to the area.

Peck had a dream of a national organization that would promote and raise funds for a frontier missionary effort and support the establishment of schools and work among the Indians. He was a tireless fund-raiser and promoter, and finally, in 1832, his dream became reality when the American Baptist Home Mission Society was established in New York City under his leadership. Its motto was "North America for Christ," and, during its first year, it sponsored 50 missions in ten states, two territories, and Canada. Within four years that number had doubled and, by the end of the decade, the society's efforts had reaped nearly 11,000 converts on the frontier and established 400 churches pastored by 142 ministers. In addition, many benevolent societies, Sunday schools, and Bible classes also had been established. Peck and the Home Mission Society had laid the groundwork for a vast home missionary enterprise that eventually would embrace the entire continent.

Peck's interest in evangelical efforts among the Indians was not wholeheartedly shared by others. Many Baptist settlers had ambivalent feelings: while they felt they had a moral obligation to save the souls of the "heathen" Indians, they and others were also eager to take over Indian lands by fair means, or, where necessary, foul means. As a result many of the early missionaries among the Indians had to struggle to gain funds to support their efforts.

From the outset, Baptists had been sympathetic to the American Indian, perhaps because the Indians also had suffered abuse and persecution. Roger Williams had championed the cause of the Narragansett Indians as did others. In 1694 an Indian Baptist church had been founded at Gay Head in Martha's Vineyard, Massachusetts. It was not until the western territories were opened in the nineteenth century, however, that Baptists began an active, organized missionary effort among Native Americans.

Many Baptists felt that bringing the Gospel to the Indians was the beginning of a civilizing process. In 1822 a Baptist Committee on Indian Missions stated that it "anticipated a period not far distant when the Indians shall be brought not merely to unite with the white man in worship of God, but to cooperate with them in the business of agriculture and trade."

While there were many evangelizing among the various Indian tribes, it was Isaac McCoy (1784-1846) who was to be the real inspiration for the Baptist missionary effort among the Indians. Born in Pennsylvania, he emigrated to Kentucky in 1790 and later converted to the Baptist faith while living in Indiana. Although self-taught, he was ordained a minister in 1810 and almost at once took up the cause of the American Indian.

Although McCoy's work initially was overshadowed by the work of Peck and others, he gained prominence when, in 1820, he founded an Indian school in Fort

Wayne, Indiana, and two years later, founded a mission near Niles, Michigan. He also established the first Baptist church in the Creek (Muskogee) Nation in 1832, and in 1842 he launched the American Indian Mission Association. McCoy is best remembererd, however, as one of the chief architects of the government's reservation system for the Indians.

McCoy devised a grand plan whereby all Indians would be resettled in a special colony beyond the frontier, assigned individual plantations, and become beneficiaries of the best civilizing and Christianizing efforts of all Protestant denominations. He lobbied vigorously for his plan, making ten trips to the nation's capital. His plan was eventually—and unfortunately—modified and absorbed into the government's program for forced removal of all Indians to specially designated lands beyond the Mississippi.

Although the Indian removal plan never was successful and was bitterly resented by the Indians, the 1852 *Annual Report of the American Baptist Missionary Union* optimistically stated that

> thousands of Indians who once roamed through forests in quest of a precarious subsistence have been reduced and won over to habits of sober and regular industry, cultivating the soil with the skill of Christian civilization and depending on its products for a more sure support. And what is of infinitely greater account, many of these have been brought to know, to love, and to obey the Savior, and to enjoy the hope of the regenerate child of God.

Baptists had greater success with the Indians than other denominations because of their policy of training Indians to serve as ministers to their own people. Evangelical efforts among the Indians were severely curtailed, however, by the Civil War, and were only revived in the late nineteenth century when new missions were established among the Creeks, Blankets, Wichitas, Caddoes, Kiowas, Comanches, Cheyennes, and Arapahoes.

The western frontier was not the only fertile territory for domestic Baptist evangelism, however. Wave after wave of foreign immigrants were ripe for evangelizing in the eastern cities. Baptist missionaries worked among the Swedish, German, and other nationalities, converting them and helping them to establish their own churches and to adjust to the customs and language of their new home while maintaining their cultural identities. Many members of these congregations often carried the Baptist message back to their native countries, aiding and joining in the burgeoning Baptist foreign missionary movement that had started, in the United States, in 1812 when Luther Rice and Ann and Adoniram Judson first set foot in India.

Luther Rice (1783–1836) was, like Peck, a man who recognized the need for a formal organization to support missions on both national and international levels. Rice grew up on a farm in Massachusetts, one of several children. He did well at school, and in 1811 he graduated from the Andover Theological Seminary as a Congregationalist minister, convinced that his future lay in foreign missionary work. So determined was he that in 1812 he paid his own way to be one of a group of Congregationalists sent by the American Board of Commissioners for Foreign Missions to India. During the sea voyage, which was rough and arduous, Rice suffered continuously from seasickness and tried to keep his mind from his illness by studying his Bible. From these studies he came away firmly convinced of the truth of believer's baptism. He shared this belief with the rest of the group, which included Adoniram Judson and his wife, Ann. Soon after landing in Calcutta, the group was baptized at William Carey's Lall Bazaar Chapel and took up the cause of Baptist evangelizing. The Congregationalists were, understandably, not pleased by their actions. Because of political difficulties, the group was forced to leave India, but, while the others went to Burma, it was decided that Rice would return to the United States to seek support and money for their efforts as he was a most eloquent and convincing speaker.

After reluctantly returning to America, Rice toured the country and urged support and recruited missionaries for the fledgling Baptist missionary effort. Adoniram Judson wrote frequent letters home that were published in various missionary periodicals, drawing an enthusiastic response that aided Rice's work. Rice's endeavors finally were rewarded by the formation of the General Missionary Convention of the Baptist Denomination in Philadelphia in 1814. Planned by Rice, this meeting also was significant because it marked the first attempt at the formal, national organization of a Baptist denomination, bringing together as it did representatives of the various sects for a common purpose. Representatives of 115 Baptist associations attended that first meeting, and Dr. Richard Furman (1755–1825) of South Carolina was elected the convention's first president.

The Triennial Convention, as it came to be called because it met every three years, was the forerunner of the many other Baptist societies and conventions founded later in the century. It also assumed the role of the prime supporter of the rapidly growing Baptist foreign missionary enterprise for the next 30 years. In 1817 it expanded its efforts to include domestic missions and education, founding Columbian College in Washington, D. C., that same year.

Rice's job now was to collect funds for these enterprises, and for a time he was successful. But by 1822 Rice found his money-raising efforts in deep trouble. The Panic of 1819 had caused many of his financial pledges to default, and Rice found he couldn't raise enough money to support all the convention's projects. He became involved in a scheme to speculate in real estate and began to mix the accounts of Columbian College with those of the missions. His speculations, combined with his bookkeeping schemes, eventually forced Columbian College into receivership and, in 1824, the convention investigated Rice and fired him as their agent. Despite his slide from prominence, however, Rice is to be remembered for his talent for organization and his pioneering efforts on behalf of the Baptist missionary movement.

Missionaries—the bearers of Christianity and Western civilization—have been in the vanguard of every modern imperialistic venture. According to an article entitled "Influence of Missions on the Temporal Condition of the Heathen" appearing in an 1849 issue of the *Baptist Missionary Magazine*:

The office of the Gospel is to bring the heathen

nations to be . . . such as Christian nations are; to put every people under heaven on the highest platform of civilization and religion, of art and science, of learning, prosperity and usefulness, of happiness and social advancement . . . . We cannot too highly prize the influence of Christianity in promoting true civilization. We contend that a true civilization cannot exist apart from Christianity.

Although these early missionaries appear to have been sincere, if perhaps a bit misguided in their efforts to help people in foreign lands, they often laid the groundwork for future economic and political ties with Western nations. By the end of the century, the Baptist foreign missionary effort covered the world. Even after regional tensions led to a split in the convention in 1845, Baptist foreign missionary work continued uninterrupted. By 1900 the Baptist denomination as a whole had a total of 564 missionaries, 4,700 native helpers, 2,000 churches, 207,000 converts, and 11,045 schools in Africa, Asia, Europe, and North and South America. What had started with stalwart, courageous individual believers seeking to spread the Gospel had become, by 1900, a formal and growing effort throughout the world, unifying—at least in one respect—the American Baptist denomination and adding to its identity.

X

Spreading the Word: Education and Publication

DURING THE COLONIAL ERA, AMERICAN EDUCATION HAD
no formal organization and primarily was religious in
intent. Informal schools for children were organized in
the homes of their parents or of the local minister.
When, in 1647, the General Court of Massachusetts
ordered the Bay area towns with a population of 50 or
more to provide a teacher for children and bond ser-
vants, the purpose was less to "educate" as we understand education, than to promote Puritanism. Needless

to say, Baptists and their children were banned from such "schools."

Similarly, in both England and America, Baptists and other nonconformists were barred from entering the various colleges and universities. In England, Edward Terrill sought to remedy this when he established a trust in 1679 in Bristol, England, to set up the first Baptist educational institution, the Bristol Baptist Academy. As early as 1722, the Philadelphia Baptist Association was seeking recruits and donations for the support of such an academy in America, although the first significant Baptist venture into higher education did not occur until 1764 with the founding of Rhode Island College (now Brown University).

The Baptist emphasis on the divine call as the only prerequisite for the ministry, and the traditional Baptist animosity toward the educated ministry of the established churches delayed any extensive participation by the denomination in the movement for higher education initiated by other Protestant denominations during colonial times. The Baptist motto at that time was "God never called an unprepared man to preach." If one was "called" to preach, then preparation for that calling was implicit. But as the Baptists became more accepted and moved into the religious mainstream in post-revolutionary America, American Baptists began to see the advantages of a trained ministry, one better equipped to spread the Baptist message and to lead the denomination at home and abroad. A better-educated Baptist laity began to demand a ministry that it could respect, one that could keep up with the competition from other growing denominations such as the Methodists and Presbyterians. Luther Rice was a vigorous advocate of

education among the Baptists, and his attitude is reflective of the growing interest in education among most
Baptists in the early 1800s. In Rice's view an educated
ministry was the key to foreign missionary success,
among other things.

All of these factors spurred a rapid expansion of
Baptist higher education in the nineteenth century. In
1820, bolstered by the impetus of the Great Revival, the
Baptists adopted a national educational policy that had
as its goal the establishment of a college in every state
to train ministers. In some areas regional education
societies were formed to provide this training; many of
these later became colleges or seminaries. In 1830 there
were only four Baptist colleges in America. Thirty years
later, Baptists were well on their way to achieving the
goal of a college in every state, with some 25 colleges
and universities.

Among the best-known institutions of higher education founded by Baptists during the nineteenth century
were Waterville College (later Colby) in Maine in 1813;
Columbian College (later George Washington University) in Washington, D. C., in 1821; Newton Theological
Seminary in Massachusetts, in 1825; Furman Academy
and Theological Institute (later Furman University) in
Charleston, South Carolina, in 1827; Rock Spring Seminary in Illinois, in 1827; Granville Literary and Theological Institution (later Denison University) in Ohio,
in 1832; Mercer University in Georgia, in 1833; Manual-Labor Institute (later Franklin College) in Indiana,
in 1834; University of Richmond in Virginia, in 1840;
Baylor University in Texas, in 1845; University of
Lewisbury (later Bucknell) in Pennsylvania, in 1846;
Madison University (later Colgate) in New York, in

1846; Kalamazoo Theological Seminary in Michigan, in 1849; the University of Chicago, in 1857; and Vassar College in New York State in 1861.

The flowering of Baptist higher education did not take place without some difficulties. Since Baptists did not have a single, unified national organization, the different colleges and universities were established through the sponsorship of a variety of Baptist groups and societies whose efforts largely were uncoordinated and often conflicting. In most of the colleges and universities stress was placed upon linguistic, historical, and theological studies, and a baccalaureate degree was considered education enough for one to assume the ministry; graduate education was not considered necessary.

After the Civil War, Baptists began to see the need for a more organized course of training, and a need to change the heretofore haphazard and localized approach to higher education. In 1868, the American Baptist Education Commission was established in New York City. This was succeeded by the American Baptist Education Society in 1888. The society acted as a liaison between donors and schools and as an advisor to new colleges. It marked the first attempt by Baptists to view higher education as a national project, and it came at a time when increased philanthropy was encouraging the higher education movement. By the close of the nineteenth century, Baptists could claim 169 educational institutions (academies, colleges, and universities) with endowments and property worth an estimated $30,000,000 and enrollments exceeding 54,000 students.

Unhappily, at a time when Baptists seemed to be

growing together with the American Baptist Education Society, they also were growing apart. In the 1890s many Northern Baptists began to question the progressive curriculum of a number of schools and universities. The University of Chicago, Brown University, and Rochester and Newton seminaries were among the institutions that came under the eyes of conservative Baptist leaders. The result of this examination led to a return to traditional Baptist ideas about Scripture and polity, and a new educational system of Bible colleges was established to replace the liberal arts-theological seminary college that had existed until then. History, theology, language, and the arts were not considered necessary by conservative members of the denomination; all that was required of a minister was that he graduate from a Bible college where he had studied the Bible as thoroughly as possible.

Since 1900, however, Baptists in Great Britain and America have sought to tighten the standards for ordination.

By 1960, most mainstream Baptists began to require four years of college education plus seminary work to achieve full ordination status in the associations. . . . Still, it has been estimated that one-third to one-half of the primary pastors in Southern and Northern U. S. Baptist pastorates lacked a college degree or any seminary studies.[1]

To a great extent, this lack of formal education on the part of a number of ministers harks back to the inde-

[1] William Henry Brackney, The Baptists (New York: Greenwood Press, 1988), pp. 53–54.

pendence of the first Baptists and the voluntary nature of the denomination. Each church is a volunatry gathering of worshippers who are free to choose whom they wish as their pastor. For a central organization to require that their pastor be educated in a certain manner violates the autonomy of that particular church and is resisted strenuously by many.

Just as higher education received a shot in the arm in the 1800s as a result of the Great Revival, so, too, did the Baptist Sunday school movement. By the 1820s, children of all Protestant denominations were being sent to Sunday school. The practice, begun in England as an educational charity for factory children, was copied enthusiastically in America. The original intent was to teach reading and writing using the Bible as a text, but soon it became a means of teaching children biblical history and doctrine at a level they could understand. The Sunday school movement in America spread rapidly. By 1825, there were Sunday schools in most cities and towns in America.

The Baptists saw, as did other denominations, the Sunday school's potential as a tool for evangelism as well as religious instruction. The first such school in the nation devoted exclusively to religious instruction was organized by the Second Baptist Church of Baltimore in 1804. Baptists were strong supporters of the American Sunday School Union formed in 1824, an interdenominational lay-operated organization that produced Sunday school lesson materials. During the Civil War, when many of the regular schools in the South were disrupted, people came to rely more heavily on Sunday schools, the majority of which were operated by Baptists. On the western frontier Sunday schools grew up with the new settlements and often paved the way for the later establishment of churches.

With Sunday schools came the need for materials to be used in them. Numerous Protestant tract and publication societies were created in the nineteenth century to supply instructional literature for these growing missionary and Sunday school movements. Many of these early publishing societies were interdenominational. The American Bible Society, for example, was founded in 1816 for the purpose of producing Bibles that could be used by all Protestant denominations throughout the world. Baptists supported the society until it refused to aid them in the development of a Bible in the Bengalee language that used the word "immerse" in place of "baptize." Baptists subsequently withdrew from the society and formed their own society, the American and Foreign Bible Society.

Since the beginning of the nineteenth century, Baptists have made consistent use of the printed word for evangelization and education. In 1801 the *Baptist Analytical Repository* started publication as a vehicle of Baptist ideas. Two years later the *Massachusetts Missionary Magazine* appeared. In 1816, Luther Rice launched the publication of the *Latter Day Luminary* in Washington, D. C., which later became *The Christian Index* in 1832.

In 1824 the Baptist General Tract Society was established to publish materials for Sunday schools. The society's first periodical, the *Baptist Tract Magazine*, was published in 1827. In 1832, the society began to produce tracts for use in foreign missions, and in 1840, the society changed its name to the American Baptist Publications and Sunday School Society. During the latter half of the nineteenth century, the society launched several Sunday school periodicals, including *The Young Reaper* (1856), *The Baptist Teacher* (1870), and *Our Little Ones* (1872).

By the end of the century, nearly every state in the union had at least one Baptist publication aimed at them. These publications helped Baptists develop a sense of denomination, encouraged support for various missionary and educational endeavors, and informed Baptist thinking on the important issues of the day. But while these publications and the missionary efforts were drawing Baptists closer, other issues were in the process of dividing them.

Brother Against Brother: Splits and Schisms

ON MARCH 4, 1861, ABRAHAM LINCOLN WAS SWORN INTO the office of the presidency. On the eve of his inauguration, he faced a national crisis no president before or since has had to face: the nation was split in two over the issue of slavery. On December 20, 1860, South Carolina had repealed its ratification of the federal Constitution and announced its secession from the Union after hearing of Lincoln's impending election. Within the next two months, six other Southern states followed its example.

During his debates with Stephen A. Douglas, Lincoln repeatedly had denied that he would interfere with slavery where it already existed, and in his inaugural address, he eloquently pleaded for the preservation of the Union, saying

> The mystic chords of memory stretching from every battlefield and every patriot grave to every living heart and hearthstone all over this broad land, will yet swell the chorus of the Union, when again touched, as surely they will be, by the better angels of our nature.

In his speech, Lincoln yet again reassured the South that he would not permit interference with slavery in the states where it existed. But he also warned those states that had seceded that he would not tolerate any violent acts against the United States. It is, he said, "the declared purpose of the Union that it *will* constitutionally defend and maintain itself."

Despite Lincoln's plea for unity, the stage already had been set for the Civil War, a war that would affect all aspects of American life, turning brother against brother, setting friend against friend. For the Baptists, the issue of slavery was merely more fuel for the controversies already burning within the denomination—controversies that would lead to a divisiveness reflective of the sadly divided United States at that time.

Because of the independent nature of the Baptists, earlier disagreements over organization, doctrine, and other matters had led to the formation of a number of splinter groups before the nineteenth century. The Seventh Day Baptists, for example, organized in 1671, adhered to the idea of the seventh day as the sabbath, and had withdrawn from the other Baptist groups. Even earlier, the General Six Principle Baptists had claimed as their charter the six foundation principles laid down in Hebrews 6:1-2: repentance, faith, baptism, the laying on of hands, the resurrection of the dead, and eternal judgment. It is no surprise, therefore, that in facing some of the most explosive issues of the day, the Baptists should find themselves divided.

The first serious splits to occur among American Baptists in the nineteenth century grew from the Great Revival and revolved around the burgeoning home and foreign missionary effort. A small but vocal anti-mission minority began to make itself heard on the western frontier around 1820, basing its objections on three reasons. The first reason they put forth against any missionary efforts was doctrinal. Frontier Baptists at that time tended to be hyper-Calvinistic in their beliefs. They felt that because God already had selected those who were to be saved, missionary activity was not only unnecessary and pointless, but also an affront to God's will. They also opposed the establishment of Sunday schools and theological seminaries for the same reason.

The second reason had to do with church organization and autonomy. The anti-missioners feared that the development of strong missionary societies would lead to increased centralization of denominational authority that would, in turn, result in the loss of authority by the local churches.

Finally, the old-time frontier farmer-preacher resented and was suspicious of the new, better-educated, "professional" missionaries such as Luther Rice. As one farmer-preacher of the day said, summing up the feelings of many, "The big trees in the woods over-shadow the little ones; and these missionaries will be all great learned men, and the people will go to hear them preach, and we shall be put down. That's the objection."

When rumors began to be widely circulated along the frontier that all Baptist churches were to be taxed for the support of the missionary effort, this opposition was transformed into open rebellion. In 1819 John Taylor, a prominent anti-missioner, wrote a pamphlet entitled *Thoughts on Missions* in which he accused missionaries of being interested only in money, comparing them to horse leeches that suck the blood out of their victims. In 1830 the Apple Creek Anti-Mission Association was founded in Illinois in response to this fear of taxation. Scores of other churches followed suit, and many Baptist congregations were torn apart over the issue. The controversy proved to be a divisive factor in the Baptist denomination, giving rise, as has been mentioned, to the Two-Seed-in-the-Spirit Predestination Baptists and the Primitive Baptists who were referred to at the time as "hard-shells," "Old School," or Anti-Mission Baptists.

Even among well-educated Baptists on the East Coast, although they lacked the hyper-Calvinism of their frontier counterparts, there was a fear that the missionary movement heralded the centralization of the denomination and a loss of local autonomy. Francis Wayland, president of Brown University, defended the anti-missionary movement in 1856, saying, "The Baptists have ever believed in the entire and absolute independence of the churches . . . with the church all ecclesiastical relations of every member, are limited to the church to which he belongs."

Wayland's sentiments advocating local church protectionism echoed those that had been earlier expressed in the New Hampshire Confession of Faith issued in 1833 and enlarged upon in 1853. This Confession of Faith was to later serve as a rallying point for fundamentalists following World War I. When a doctrinal dispute erupted in the Northern Baptist Convention, two of the schismatic groups, the General Association of Regular Baptists and the Conservative Baptist Association, adopted modified versions of the 1853 confession. Similarly, in 1925, the Southern Baptist Convention adopted a statement on "Baptist Faith and Message" which was, again, based on the New Hampshire Confession of Faith. During the 1970s and 1980s, the confession has served as a basis for the fundamentalists in the Southern Baptist Convention in their attempt to implement changes in the denomination.

In addition to influencing ideas about centralization in the Baptist denomination well into the next century, the New Hampshire Confession found ready acceptance by the so-called Landmark movement within the denomination in the mid- and late-nineteenth century. Landmarkism is not a denomination among Baptists, but rather a position (sometimes viewed as heretical) concerning the nature of the church. The name is borrowed from a pamphlet written by James Madison Pendleton entitled "An Old Landmark Re-Set." Both he and James R. Graves, leader of the "Cotton Grove Convention" of the Southern Baptists in 1851, are credited with originating the Landmark movement. Graves supported the idea of the autonomy of the local church, saying that a church is "a single congregation, complete in itself, independent of all other bodies . . . and the highest and only source of ecclesiastical authority on earth, amenable only to Christ."

In addition to the belief in local church autonomy, there are three other main tenets held by Landmarkers. They believe that a valid baptism must be done only by a properly ordained Baptist clergyman and that members of other denominations or churches are not Christians; they have not been "saved" in "the true Gospel sense." Finally, Landmarkers believe that "there is a direct, historic 'succession' of Baptist churches back to New Testament times . . . ."[1] This latter view, referred to as "apostolic succession," is held by very few Baptists today outside the American Baptist Association, which evolved from the Landmark movement. The association, originally named the Baptist General Association, exerts its greatest influence in the South and today has a membership of approximately 800,000 in over 3,000 churches.

While many were protesting the missionary and fund-raising work of such people as Luther Rice or holding forth for the independence of the local church, others were trying to draw the disparate parts of the denomination into a unified whole. In the 1830s voluntary societies in New England and New York reorganized as state conventions to promote fellowship and raise funds. Similar conventions were being organ-

[1] Frank S. Mead, *Handbook of Denominations in the United States* (New York: Abingdon Press, 1965), p. 47.

ized in the South and West, following the lead of South Carolina in 1821. Representatives from the various conventions and regions were meeting every three years at the Triennial Convention. It seemed, in the early part of the century, as though perhaps a national unity of the denomination might well be on its way to completion. But this seeming unity was soon to suffer a fatal blow due to the increasing strife and controversy occasioned by that "peculiar institution"—slavery.

During colonial times Baptists were, by and large, ambivalent regarding the issue of slavery. It was a practice generally accepted at the time and many Baptists were slave owners. Most prominent Baptists were too wrapped up in the struggle for religious freedom to give much attention to the issue, and even those who genuinely were concerned about the plight of the slaves were reluctant to become involved in what they considered a civil rather than a church issue, or to interfere with what was seen as a matter of personal conscience.

However, the humanitarian and democratic spirit characterizing the Great Awakening brought the issue into sharper focus for everyone in the eighteenth century, including the Baptists. Large numbers of blacks were attracted to the Baptist denomination and many Baptists began to question the morality of Christians owning slaves. By the end of the Revolutionary War, many Baptist churches were ready to take action on the issue. In 1787 the Ketocton Association in Virginia denounced slavery as a violation of God's law and organized a committee to study ways of achieving emancipation. The committee's report drew so much opposition, however, that its proposals never were adopted.

In 1789 John Leland proposed the following resolution to the Baptist General Committee in Virginia:

> Resolved, that slavery is a violent deprivation of the rights of nature, and inconsistent with a republican government, and therefore recommend it to our brethren, to make use of every legal measure to extirpate this horrid evil from the land.

Although this resolution was adopted by the committee, no positive action ever was taken on it.

As the eighteenth century drew to a close, many Baptists, particularly in the North and the border states of Kentucky and Illinois, were coming to embrace the abolitionist cause. As new territories were opened on the frontier, controversy raged among all Americans as to whether they should be free or slave territories and states. More and more people were being asked to take a position. Among the Baptists, abolitionist preachers used their pulpits as platforms for their antislavery views, and in 1805, the Friends of Humanity Association was formed in Kentucky and later spread throughout the Midwest. Slaveholders were forbidden membership in the churches that belonged to the association, and the association later became involved in the Underground Railroad.

The issue of slavery was inflamed further by the rebellion of 70 slaves led by Nat Turner, a part-time black Baptist preacher supposedly acting on divine inspiration, as he later testified. Nat Turner was born in 1800 in Southampton County, Virginia, the property of a slave owner named Benjamin Turner. From the time he was a child, Turner had a sense of destiny. "My father and mother," he said in *The Confessions of Nat Turner*, an account recorded and published by Thomas R. Gray, "strengthened me in this my first impression, saying in my presence, I was intended for some great purpose, which they had always thought from certain marks on my head and breast." Turner's parents taught him to read and taught him the Bible, imbuing him with a feeling that God had some great purpose for him.

In 1824 or 1825 Turner escaped from his master and fled to the woods after receiving a savage flogging from the overseer. While in the woods he decided to return to slavery but, "about this time," he told Gray,

> I had a vision—and I saw white spirits and black spirits engaged in battle, and the sun was darkened—the thunder rolled in the Heavens, and blood flowed in streams—and I heard a voice saying, "Such is your luck, such you are called to see, and let it come rough or smooth, you must surely bear it."

Turner felt he had been shown that there would be a bloody war to set slaves free and that he and his chosen followers were to undertake it.

In 1825 Turner returned to his master's plantation and began secretly to plan and organize his fellow slaves in the struggle for freedom. During that time he saw what he felt were other divine signs. After a partial eclipse of the sun on February 12, 1831, Turner finally felt able to tell his companions of his plan; the eclipse was, he felt, a sign from God to do so. On Sunday, August 20, 1831, Turner led his companions in rebellion. Over 60 whites were killed before the rebels were crushed. A wave of hysteria washed over all the slaveholding states where slave owners knew that the rebellion was the inevitable fruit to be harvested from the years of bloodshed and oppression. Among slaveholders fear of rebellion reached new heights and there was an increased feeling of defensiveness about an institution that had become economically vital to the South.

Among the Baptists the issue of slavery came to a head in the 1840s, causing a split between Baptists along Northern and Southern lines that persists to this day. For years there had been mounting tension between the Northern and Southern members of the Triennial Convention. Many Southern Baptists felt that Baptists from the North dominated the convention and ignored Southern concerns. The growing abolitionist sentiment among Northern Baptists aggravated the resentment of the Southern members and put them even more on the defensive regarding slavery than they were already. When an American Baptist Anti-Slavery Convention met in New York in 1840, Southern Baptists were outraged. Many Southern churches, fearful that "radical abolitionists" were about to take over the Triennial Convention's missionary societies, withheld funds from them. The moderate leaders of the convention did their utmost to reassure the Southern membership, and at the Triennial Convention's meeting in Philadelphia in April 1844, a resolution was passed as a concession to the South. It stated

That in co-operating together as members of this Convention in the work of foreign missions, we disclaim all sanction either express or implied, whether slavery or anti-slavery, but as individuals we are perfectly free both to express and promote our various views on these subjects in a Christian manner and spirit.

When the Alabama State Convention decided to test the sincerity of the convention's leaders by demanding that the Triennial Convention allow slaveholders to act as missionaries, the abolitionist sentiment of the Northern members ultimately prevailed. In December 1844, the Board of Managers of the Triennial Convention issued the following statement:

If any one should offer himself as a missionary, having slaves, and should insist on retaining them as his property, we could not appoint him. One thing is certain, we can never be a party to any arrangement which would imply approbation of slavery.

With the position of the Triennial Convention so baldly clarified, the Southern states felt they had no other option but to disassociate themselves from the convention. The Alabama State Convention was the first to express these feelings, but it was quickly followed by eleven other Southern states. Representatives of nearly 300 Southern congregations then met in Augusta, Georgia, in May 1845, to form the Southern Baptist Convention. That year there were 351,951 members in the convention. The division within the denomination reflected the growing division between North and South in the United States as a whole, a split that would not be healed for decades. With the outbreak of

the Civil War in 1861, the North-South split between
the Baptists deepened. Baptists in the North supported
the Union cause, not merely because of its antislavery
position, but because of their desire to defend a democratic government that guaranteed religious and political freedom as well. Northern ministers exhorted their
congregations to support the cause, raising funds and
serving in the ranks of the Union Army as soldiers,
chaplains, and medics. In this they were joined by
black Baptists from both the North and South.

A resolution passed at the Southern Baptist Convention's meeting in 1861, on the other hand, leaves no
doubt where the loyalties of Southern Baptists lay:

> That we most cordially approve of the formation of
> the Government of the Confederate States of Amer-
> ica, and admire and applaud the noble cause of
> that government up to the present time . . . every
> principle of religion, of patriotism, and of human-
> ity calls upon us to pledge our fortunes and lives
> in the good work.

The Civil War raged for four bloody years until the
surrender of General Robert E. Lee at Appomattox
Courthouse on April 9, 1865. The Confederacy was
dead but the North-South split continued. The North
had suffered lightly during the war and was on the road
to prosperity due to increased industrialization. The
South, however, lay in ruins. Even six years after the
war, Robert Somers, an English traveler wrote that

> . . . [the South] consists for the most part of planta-
> tions in a state of semi-ruin, and plantations of

which the ruin is for the present total and complete . . . . The trial of war is visible throughout
the valley in burnt-up gin houses, ruined bridges,
mills and factories . . . and in large tracts of once-
cultivated land stripped of every vestige of fenc-
ing.

For the Baptists, the split between North and South
precipitated by the slavery issues and the issue of local
church authority, was irreparable. While Northern and
Southern states struggled to recover and reunite, Northern and Southern Baptist conventions grew even more
independent of one another. Today the Southern Baptist Convention is the largest and fastest-growing Protestant denomination in America, far outnumbering its
Northern counterpart in members and even expanding
its own membership into Northern states. What the
Civil War precipitated is now an organization that is
far-reaching and formidable in its influence.

XII

"Shall We Gather at the River?": The Modern Baptist Conventions

AFTER THE BLOODSHED, STRIFE, AND DIVISIVENESS OF THE
Civil War, Americans—both Southern and Northern—
yearned for peace and a restoration of unity. In 1864 the
Reverend Robert Loury, a well-known composer of sacred songs, reflected this desire in his *Shall We Gather
at the River?*, one of the classic Baptist hymns:

Shall we gather at the river,
Where bright angel feet have trod,
With its crystal tides forever
Flowing by the throne of God?

But just as the war-torn United States was suffering
from the disjointedness of the times, so, too, were the
Baptists suffering from a separation of factions. The
dispute over the slavery issue may have precipitated
the final break between Northern and Southern Baptists, but there had been other factors contributing to
that division—a division that became permanent as the
twentieth century loomed on the horizon.

One of the major differences between Northern and
Southern Baptists concerned their approaches to denominational structure and administration. Baptists of
the North shied away from any strong, centralized
church administration, although they were willing to
support the cooperative efforts of several separate, independent societies such as the American Baptist
Home Mission Society and the American Baptist Publication Society. After the Southern Baptists seceded
from the Triennial Convention in 1845, the Northern
Baptists renamed the convention the American Baptist
Missionary Union and later, the American Baptist Foreign Mission Society. This society, along with the
American Baptist Home Mission Society and American
Baptist Publication Society, served as a loose organizational unit for the Northern Baptists. Although the
three bodies were separate corporations, they often
called annual meetings at the same place and time. In
addition, several new, independent societies came into
being that reflected the changing needs and influences

of the times. Prominent among these were the Women's American Baptist Foreign Mission Societies (1871), the Women's American Baptist Home Mission Societies (1877), the American Baptist Education Society (1888), and the Baptist Young People's Union (1891).

By the turn of the century, however, it was becoming increasingly apparent that the society method was no longer a practical way of administering denominational affairs. Having so many independent societies competing with one another for funding and membership was creating confusion and proving to be wasteful and a detriment to the overall mission of Northern Baptists. So in 1907, the Northern Baptist Convention was formed to coordinate the efforts of the various national societies, state conventions, and regional associations. Each agency within the Northern Baptist Convention retained its autonomy, the convention declaring from the start "its belief in the independence of the local church, and in the purely advisory nature of all denominational organizations composed of representative churches." The convention was restricted in its powers to conduct religious works and receive and spend money, thus safeguarding the independence of the local churches.

In 1950 the Northern Baptist Convention's name was changed to the American Baptist Convention and in 1972, in a reorganizational move, it was changed yet again to the American Baptist Churches in the U.S.A. Today a General Board oversees the various activities of the separate Boards of Educational Ministries, International Ministries, National Ministries, and a Ministers and Missionaries Benefit Board. The General Board is comprised of elected representatives from election districts rather than from individual churches or associations. Headquartered in Valley Forge, Pennsylvania, the organization holds annual meetings.

Baptists belonging to the American Baptist Churches in the U.S.A. tend to be more liberal in their beliefs than their Southern counterparts. As was their desire from the start, in matters of faith each church is autonomous, although they do hold certain beliefs in common. The Bible is, of course, the foundation of their belief and the individual's conscience is the interpreter of the Bible. The ordinances of baptism and the Lord's Supper (communion), however, are considered more as aids than as necessities to the living of a Christian life. Membership today in the American Baptist Churches in the U.S.A. numbers over 1,500,000 in over 5,000 congregations.

The desire for freedom from a central organization and a liberalism in thought and theology separated the Northern from the Southern Baptists even before the Civil War and the issue of slavery brought these differences to a head. While Northern Baptists shied away from a controlling, centralized church organization, Southern Baptists favored a strong, unifying administration—and from its beginning the Southern Baptist Convention (SBC) was just such an organization. William B. Johnson (1782-1862), the first president of the SBC, according to the proceedings of the SBC's first convention held in May 1845 in Augusta, Georgia, oversaw a plan to "elicit, combine, and direct the energies of the whole denomination in one sacred effort." Within the SBC, five denominational boards assumed the work that previously had been assigned to societies in the North: the Home Mission Board, the Foreign

Mission Board, the Sunday School Board, the Annuity Board, and the Publications Board.

The early years of the Southern Baptist Convention were difficult ones. The Civil War badly wounded the South and its effects were felt in the small, fledgling organization, but the convention recovered rapidly and by 1890 had 1,235,908 members. Instead of delegates limited to and elected by associations, the SBC invited all churches that contributed at least $100 yearly to send delegates, insuring direct participation by the individual churches. State conventions, associations, and churches all had, and continue to have today, an equal footing in the convention delegations.

Today the SBC is the largest and fastest-growing Protestant denomination in America, far outnumbering its Northern equivalent with a membership of over 14,500,000 in over 36,000 churches. The convention headquarters is in Nashville, Tennessee, and its annual convention draws members from Northern and Western states equally, as well as from the South. Although still named the *Southern* Baptist Convention, the organization's influence has spread throughout the United States, its members joined by a commonality of belief.

Southern Baptists are more conservative in their beliefs than members of the American Baptist Churches in the U.S.A. The Southern brand of Baptist faith tends to be more Calvinistic, and the SBC adheres firmly (and ironically) to the New Hampshire Confession of Faith. Because it began when the members of the SBC drew together to confront a common enemy—the North—the SBC has maintained a strong organization and experienced little dissension in the ranks over the years. In the 1970s, however, conflict was to raise its head, leading to disagreement and splits within what had been until then one of the most unified denominations in America. The disagreement was to be, once again, over an issue that had time and again raised its head during the history of the Baptists: freedom.

The issue of freedom had assumed a different meaning for black Baptists before and after the Civil War. For black Baptists the battle was not only individual freedom to worship, but also personal freedom. After over 200 years of slavery and oppression, the Civil War and the passage of the Thirteenth Amendment to the Constitution in 1865 had granted personal freedom to blacks. But the struggle for the equal right to enjoy that freedom was a battle just beginning.

The first shipload of African slaves arrived in Jamestown in 1619, one year before the *Mayflower* brought the Pilgrims to Plymouth, and for the next 200 years the slave trade brought a steady influx of blacks to America. Initially, colonial slave owners didn't concern themselves with the religious education of their slaves, and in the latter half of the seventeenth century, after several English courts declared that baptized slaves must be freed, slave owners openly opposed conversion of their slaves. Later, after many of the colonies passed legislation declaring that baptism did not automatically confer the right to freedom, many slave owners relaxed their opposition. It took the Great Awakening, however, to spur white Americans to the conversion of blacks to Christianity.

As has been mentioned, many blacks were drawn to the Baptist faith because of the simplicity of its message, its emotional appeal, and its democratic organization; there was no reluctance to ordain black ministers.

Baptists actively evangelized among black slaves, and from the start, blacks were admitted into white churches. Slaves usually attended the churches of their masters, where they were segregated in a gallery of their own. White ministers also traveled to plantations and ministered to the slaves, sometimes with the assistance of a black helper who often was an ordained minister himself. As the Baptist faith spread among the slaves, black churches were also established. By 1800 there were over 25,000 black Baptists in the United States, representing approximately one-quarter of all blacks in the nation.

In the early part of the nineteenth century, more black congregations were formed in Massachusetts, Pennsylvania, Ohio, Illinois, and New York. In 1808, for example, the Abyssinian Baptist Church was founded in New York City. It was destined to become the largest Baptist congregation in the world more than a century later under the leadership of the Reverend Adam Clayton Powell.

Before the North-South split in 1845, black Baptists participated along with whites in the Triennial Convention, pursuing the same goals as white Baptists, evangelizing, and doing missionary work. The first modern Baptist missionary to work outside his own country was a black man. In 1783 the threat of re-enslavement forced George Leile (c. 1750-c. 1800), a former slave who had been freed by his master, Henry Sharpe, in Georgia, to flee the country. His missionary work in Jamaica predated William Carey's by over a decade and that of Adoniram Judson and Luther Rice by 30 years. While in Jamaica Leile founded the First African Baptist Church of Kingston and influenced later missionaries to return to England and support the abolitionist movement there.

In 1815, just one year after the formation of the Triennial Convention, blacks founded their own missionary society in Richmond, Virginia, under the leadership of Lott Carey (c. 1780-1829), a former slave who had purchased his freedom and that of his children for $850. After purchasing his freedom Carey had learned to read and write at William Crane's night school for blacks and attended the First Baptist Church in Richmond, Virginia, where he was baptized in 1807. After his baptism, Carey worked with the First African Baptist Church in Richmond, and it was this work that led to the formation of the Richmond African Missionary Society in 1815. In 1821 the society, along with both the American Colonization Society and the American Baptist Board of Foreign Missions, sent Carey and Collin Teague to Liberia, where they established the Providence Baptist Church in Monrovia.

By 1845 black Baptists made up a significant portion of the Baptist denomination. When Southern Baptists split with the Triennial Convention, many black Baptists initially went with them. In 1845 there were 351,951 members in the Southern Baptist Convention, of whom 130,000 were black. The issue of slavery and race, however, again caused dissension. The black Baptists withdrew from the SBC to form their own convention; by 1890 there were 1,235,908 members in the Southern Baptist Convention, none of whom were black.

The first black Baptist association, the Providence Baptist Association of Ohio, had been formed in 1836. After the Civil War a revival swept the black population and created thousands of new churches. Helped by the Freedman's Aid Society and missionaries from larger Baptist denominations, nearly 1,000,000 black Baptists were worshipping in their own churches by 1880. This spurt of growth started a movement among black Baptists to organize on all levels. The first state convention had been held in North Carolina in 1866. This quickly had been followed by conventions in Alabama (1866), Virginia (1867), Arkansas (1868), Kentucky (1869), and Georgia (1870). A number of attempts at national organization also were made. The first black Baptist national organization centered around missionary efforts; the American Baptist Missionary Convention was organized at the Abyssinian Baptist Church in New York City in 1860. This was followed in 1864 by the Western and Southern Missionary Baptist Conventions. The two groups merged in 1866 to form the Consolidated American Baptist Missionary Convention.

In 1880 the Foreign Mission Baptist Convention was launched by the Reverend Colley in Montgomery, Alabama. It soon was followed, in 1886, by the American National Baptist Convention, organized in St. Louis, and in 1893 by the National Baptist Educational Convention, founded in the District of Columbia. All three of these conventions merged in 1895 to form the National Baptist Convention, U.S.A., the first fully cooperative national effort at organization among black Baptists.

In 1915 a rift developed within the National Baptist Convention over the adoption of a charter and the ownership of a publishing house. The group accepting the charter became known as the National Baptist Convention of the U.S.A., Incorporated. Today it is the largest black Baptist convention, with a membership of over 5,500,000 in 26,000 churches.

The group rejecting the charter became known as the National Baptist Convention of America, Unincorporated. Organized in 1915 by Richard H. Boyd (1843-1922), its membership numbers nearly 3,000,000 in 11,398 congregations.

While these are the two largest black Baptist conventions, other smaller conventions exist geared to the particular needs and beliefs of their members. In 1907, for example, the National Primitive Baptist Convention of the U.S.A. was founded (formerly Colored Primitive Baptists). While their doctrine and theology are the same as in the white Primitive churches, the organization is ironically "opposed to all forms of church organization," although there are local associations and the National Primitive Baptist Convention holds meetings. The United Free Will Baptist Church was organized in 1901 as an organization of black Free Will Baptists, and in 1961, the Progressive National Baptist Convention, Inc. was founded with the help of Martin Luther King, Jr., as a reform group within the National Baptist Convention in the U.S.A.

Blacks now also are represented within the major, predominantly white conventions. After the Civil War both the Northern Baptist Convention and the Southern Baptist Convention carried on missionary work among black freedmen of the South. Many of those converted to the Baptist faith chose to work within the predominantly white organizations, feeling that this was a means of achieving greater understanding. By 1900, however, the major conventions of the Baptist denomination were in place. Within a denomination that in its infancy had resisted all ideas of centralized organization, there now were, ironically, a number of strong groups that cooperated with one another, coordinated the efforts of their various churches, and were ready to face the challenges and problems of the new century.

XIII

The Twentieth Century: Science, Modernism, and "That Old Time Religion"

IN THE DECADES FOLLOWING THE CIVIL WAR, AMERICA AND the rest of the Western world underwent an intellectual, economic, and social revolution that was to have a profound effect on religious thought and activity throughout the next century. It was an age in which scientific discoveries were to alter the ways man viewed his place in the world, and, even more significantly, his relationship with God. It also was a time when the fruits of the industrial revolution and the rapid development of America's natural resources were making life more comfortable for a majority of Americans and veritably luxurious for those who were their major exploiters—the leaders of "Big Business," the oil barons, the steel tycoons, and the railroad kings.

This new devotion to scientific rationalism and material pursuits contributed to the general decline in spirituality that occurred in America at this time and manifested itself in the growing secularization of religion and formalization of worship. However, among the better-educated ministers in American religious circles, nothing was more disruptive than the advent of Darwinism. When Charles Darwin set forth his theory of evolution in his *On the Origin of Species*, published in England in 1859, he had no way of forecasting the conflicts his theory would generate among theologians—not only in the remaining decades of the nineteenth century but throughout the twentieth century.

The first response by clergymen to the challenge of evolution was an almost unanimous rejection of the concept as atheistic materialism. But Darwinism could not be shoved into a dark corner and forgotten. Increasingly the clergy were being asked to confront and answer Darwin, or at least to somehow resolve his theories in respect to the Bible. Many Protestant theologians readily accepted Darwin's theory and adapted their interpretation of the Bible to accommodate it. These scholars cast aside the strict Calvinism characteristic of traditional Protestant thought in favor of a more liberal, democratic, and progressive view of man's relationship to God. Henry Ward Beecher, for example, told his congregation that evolution was the "deciphering of God's thought as revealed in the structure of the world." Lyman Abbott, another outstanding minister of the 1880s, wrote that "God is not merely a 'Great First Cause,' but the one Great Cause from whom all forms of nature and life continuously proceed." In other words, for Abbott and others, Darwinism provided evidence of the infinite wisdom of God.

For the Baptists, Darwin and this theory of evolution had and was to continue to have profound and far-reaching consequences. A majority of Baptists were shocked by the new, liberal theology that attempted to accommodate evolution. Proponents of this orthodox school held that "the author of the Bible is the Holy Spirit," and, as proof, pointed to the unity the Bible claimed for itself. One of the strongest supporters of this view was Adoniram Judson Gordon (1836-1895), pastor of the Clarendon Street Baptist Church of Boston. Gordon denied any validity whatsoever to the theory of evolution and, rather, stressed the literal truth of the Bible and that the church's role was to save men's souls and prepare them for the kingdom of heaven. Gordon's studies of the Bible eventually led him to the belief in the imminent Second Coming of Christ. In 1878 he began publication of a periodical entitled *The Watchword* to publicize these chiliastic concerns.

While Gordon and other conservatives were combating the advances in scientific thought and their application to the Bible, other Baptists were embracing a "modernist" approach. Prominent among them was Walter Rauschenbusch (1861-1918), one of the leading

Baptist proponents of the "Social Gospel" or "Christian Socialism."

Walter Rauschenbusch was born and raised in Rochester, New York, the son of a German immigrant Baptist pastor, August Rauschenbusch, who had pioneered the German Baptist Conference in America. Walter Rauschenbusch's first assignment as a pastor was to the notorious Hell's Kitchen area of New York City. This was to influence his thoughts for the rest of his life. It was there that he began to develop the convictions that would crystallize into the Social Gospel movement during his subsequent tenure as professor of church history at the Rochester Theological Seminary. He was moved deeply by the daily hardship and suffering of the urban poor, and he felt that the church had a responsibility to work for the improvement of conditions in places such as Hell's Kitchen. Changes, he believed, could be achieved by the universal application of the teachings of Jesus, and only under a cooperative economic system that allowed everyone an equal share could God's kingdom be realized.

Rauschenbusch spent his life seeking out and publishing theological and biblical precedents for his radical reform theories. His first book, *Christianity and Social Crisis*, published in 1907, pointed out the repeated concern for the poor and oppressed expressed in the Bible. In the preface to that book, he wrote that "the essential purpose of Christianity was to transform human society into the Kingdom of God by regenerating all human relations and reconstituting them in accordance with the Will of God." Rauschenbusch is perhaps best known for his book, *A Theology for the Social Gospel*, in which he describes his perception of the kingdom of God as "humanity organized according to the Will of God." Years later, Martin Luther King, Jr., was to acknowledge the influence Rauschenbusch had on his thinking.

Rauschenbusch was but one of a number of scholars, educators, and pastors who espoused the liberal, modernist approach. Others included William N. Clarke, William H. P. Faunce, and George D. Boardman, Jr., all of whom stressed the importance of the New Testament over the Old Testament and the interpretive nature of the Bible as a whole. Boardman, pastor of the First Baptist Church of Philadelphia and a stepson of Adoniram Judson, one of the first Baptist missionaries, summed up the thoughts of many of the modernists when he wrote, "I do not believe that the Creation Record [in the Bible] is to be taken literally. The words describing Creation are figurative or parabolic."

The majority of Baptists, particularly in the South, rejected Rauschenbusch's Social Gospel and the entire modernist movement in favor of a more traditional and conservative Protestant doctrine. In the South, where the Southern Baptist Convention had its power base, conservative Baptists had no problem. In the North, however, conservatives felt they had to combat the growing liberal trend. Beginning in 1910, conservatives began a campaign for the investigation of liberal teachings in church-affiliated schools, and to found schools, conservative in orientation, in response to what they felt was the creeping liberalism within the already established schools. For example, in 1913 the Northern Theological Seminary in Chicago was founded to train a conservative ministry to offset the liberalism of the University of Chicago Divinity School.

The battle between conservatives and liberals came to a head at the 1920 annual meeting of the Northern Baptist Convention. Under the leadership of Jasper C. Massee, the conservatives focused on the issue of the "false teachings in Baptist schools." It was proposed that existing schools be examined and tested for orthodoxy. Massee and his followers proposed to use as a guideline the New Hampshire Confession of Faith that declared that the Bible was "divinely inspired . . . a perfect treasure . . . without any mixture of error."

While the fundamentalists carried the day at the 1920 meeting, the proposal to examine schools met with incomplete success. The advocates of the proposal argued over the evaluative procedure and, when questionnaires were sent out, most were not returned. Most college administrators shared the feeling of William H. P. Faunce, president of Brown University, that they must "stand fast in the soul liberty of Roger Williams." The most detrimental effect the proposal had was a gradual loosening of ties between the denomination and schools such as Colgate, Colby, Bates, and Rochester Universities, all of which would completely sever those ties by 1950.

The fundamentalists were not finished, however, and in 1922 attempted to have the Northern Baptist Convention vote in favor of adoption of the New Hampshire Confession of Faith and, for the first time, talked of biblical inerrancy (the belief that the Bible is the literal truth dictated by the Holy Spirit). The notion of biblical inerrancy was and continues to be an issue hotly debated within the denomination. For the Southern Baptist Convention, it is one that was to assume "biblical" proportions in the 1980s. For the Northern Baptist Convention, the more liberal members won out in the 1920s and the issue has not reemerged.

The most significant result of the controversy was the formation of the Baptist Bible Union in 1923. Conservative leaders from the Northern, Southern, and Canadian conventions met in Kansas City, Missouri, in 1923 to create an organization to combat modernism, to create "a union of all Baptists who believe the Bible to be the Word of God." It was at this meeting that Curtis Lee Laws, editor of the *Watchman-Examiner*, coined the term "fundamentalist." At their meeting, Union members adopted a modified New Hampshire Confession of Faith and publicly advised their churches against supporting any institution advocating modernism:

> Members are encouraged absolutely to refuse longer to contribute money to an educational institution or missionary organization which refuses to avow this allegiance to the fundamentals of the faith.

The "Battle for the Bible" aside, however, evangelical Protestants during the first half of the twentieth century for the most part were aware of the need to rise to the challenges of the social, intellectual, and economic changes America and the world were undergoing. It was no longer merely enough to spread the Gospel and win converts to Christ. It also was necessary to minister to the whole person and to help him further his growth as a Christian in a rapidly changing and often confusing world. One result was that most denominations began to weigh the benefits of working in closer cooperation with one another. This ecumenical movement led to the formation of a number of cooperative Protestant organizations, including the Federal Council of the Churches of Christ in America in 1908 (later the National Council of the Churches of Christ in the U.S.A., in 1950), and on the international level, the World Council of Churches in 1948.

While other denominations were joining these ecumenical groups, the Baptists were divided in their participation. The Northern Baptist Convention joined both groups at the start. The Southern Baptist Convention, however, consistently has refused to participate in either.

Baptists launched their own worldwide movement in 1905 with the formation of the Baptist World Alliance in London. Baptists from 23 nations attended the Alliance's inaugural meeting. Its goals, formulated at that meeting, are the promotion of worldwide fellowship and cooperation among Baptists, greater understanding between Baptists and other Christians, the Gospel of Chirst, peace among men, alleviation of human suffering, missionary cooperation, religious liberty, and human rights. Today nearly 90 percent of the world's Baptists are represented in the Baptist World Alliance.

Cooperation among Baptists and between Baptists and other denominations was necessary, it was felt, during the first half of the twentieth century, a period of worldwide social and political upheaval. Two wars and a devastating economic depression turned the world upside down and left permanent scars on the human spirit. Almost daily, it seemed, advances in science and technology were changing everyday life in dramatic ways. It was the age of the automobile and airplane, radio, motion pictures, and finally, television, all of which shrank the world into a "global village."

Evangelism continued to be the number-one priority among American Baptists during the first half of the twentieth century, and the missionary and educational enterprises of both the Northern and Southern Baptist Conventions grew steadily despite setbacks within the conventions. The Spanish-American War had increased greatly the foreign holdings of the United States. America's churches wasted no time in staking their claims to the new territories. In fact, on July 13, 1898, even before the war had ended, missionaries from several Protestant denominations met in New York City to divide up Puerto Rico, Cuba, and the Philippines. The chairman of the meeting was S. W. Duncan, secretary of the American Baptist Missionary Union. This meeting laid the groundwork for the interdenominational cooperation that characterized much of the Protestant missionary activity after 1900.

There were many Baptists, however, who felt that America's overseas intervention was unjust and unconstitutional and they wanted no part of it. These views found a forum in two of the most influential Baptist periodicals of the day, the *Baptist Standard* and the *Watchman-Examiner*.

In the years preceding World War I, Baptists enthusiastically cultivated their new mission fields and continued to expand their already established influence in Asia, Africa, and Europe. The destruction of mission property and interruption of the flow of funds to missions caused by World War I led to a temporary decline in Baptist missionary activity, but after the Armistice was signed in 1918, missionary efforts picked up again. A massive nationwide fund-raising campaign, called the New World Movement, was launched by the Northern Baptist Convention after the war. In addition to raising $50,000,000 in four years, the movement also increased the laity's awareness of and support for foreign missionary activities.

This upsurge in foreign missionary activity was curtailed by the Great Depression and the threat of another war. Japan's invasion of China, for example, caused the destruction of much Baptist mission property, including the University of Shanghai. As the war in the Pacific broadened, so did the destruction of Baptist missions in Burma, Assam, and the Philippines. Scores of Baptist missionaries were imprisoned by the Japanese for the duration of the war. American missionaries were recalled from Japan, and the Japanese took over the leadership of the Baptist church there. After the war Baptists once again returned to these war-torn countries and set about rebuilding the missions that had been destroyed in both Asia and Europe.

The events of the first half of the twentieth century affected not only Baptist missionary efforts abroad but also Baptists at home. Since the days of the American Revolution, Baptists had been strong supporters of the American government. When President Wilson decided that America should enter the hostilities in Europe in 1917, the Baptist churches in America supported his decision. That same year the Northern Baptist Convention passed a resolution pledging "to the President and government of the United States our wholehearted support." Baptists used their pulpits to generate support for what they considered a just, even holy war. After the war, when America pursued a policy of isolation at home and abroad, Baptists supported the government again by advocating disarmament and by participating in the League of Nations and Court of International Justice.

This total acceptance of American policy was to come to an end during the Depression. Several issues caused Baptist leaders to rethink their attitudes. During the Depression a number of Baptist leaders became uneasy about the social programs instituted by the New Deal, seeing in them an assumption by the government of the philanthropic activities of the churches. In 1937 both Northern and Southern Baptist Conventions joined together to urge the government to investigate the persecution of Christians in Rumania. What brought the Baptist denomination together in opposition to the government, ultimately, were President Franklin Roosevelt's appointment in 1939 of Myron C. Taylor as a representative to the Vatican and the governmental funding of graduate education in parochial institutions through the National Youth Administration. To many Baptists these two things heralded an unhealthy breakdown of the separation of church and state. In 1939, in an unusual show of unity, representatives from both Southern and Northern Baptist Conventions met to form what became known, in 1941, as the Baptist Joint Committee on Public Affairs. The committee envisioned its function as being

—to keep Baptists informed on public affairs;
—to compile, analyze and disseminate data on public issues and legislative, judicial and administrative policy, and

—to inform the government of Baptist positions on issues relevant to public policy.

Joseph M. Dawson, the committee's first executive director, was a shrewd politician and lobbyist. The first issue the committee tackled was Myron Taylor's appointment to the Vatican. As Rufus W. Weaver, a spokesperson for the Baptists and pastor at First Baptist Church in Washington, D.C., put it,

> The distinctive theory upon which this government has been founded is the absolute separation of church and state, and any recognition, implied or otherwise, of the political status of any ecclesiastical organization constitutes, in our judgment, an assault upon this principle.

In spite of widespread support for this position from other evangelical Protestants, the president sent Taylor anyway, and aid to parochial institutions continued. However, in 1951, Baptist lobbying helped defeat proposed legislation that would have appointed a full ambassador to the Vatican. The Joint Committee was more successful on the issue of the persecution of Rumanian Christians and through diplomatic channels won for them freedom from persecution.

Since its formation the Joint Committee has upheld the Baptists' long tradition of supporting religious liberty and the separation of church and state. In a statement issued in 1944, the committee outlined its position: "We believe that religious liberty is the ultimate ground of democratic institutions, and that wherever this liberty is questioned, restricted, or denied by any group—political, religious or philosophical—all other human rights are impaired."

Human rights was to become an issue when at the Baptist World Alliance meeting in Berlin in 1934, Baptists came face to face with the most deadly menace to peace the world had known until then: Adolf Hitler and the Nazi movement. One response was the adoption at the 1939 annual meetings of the Northern, National, and Southern Baptist Conventions of the "American Baptist Bill of Rights." Noting the "sudden rise of European dictators" and "special favors extended to certain ecclesiastical bodies," (this in reference to Roosevelt's appointment of Taylor and the parochial schools issue), the Bill of Rights asserted that "no issue in modern life is more urgent than the relation of organized religion to organized society." "A Baptist," the bill further stated, "must exercise himself to the utmost in the maintenance of absolute religious liberty for his Jewish neighbor, his Catholic neighbor, his Protestant neighbor, and for everyone else." With the Japanese attack on Pearl Harbor on December 7, 1941, most American Baptists wholeheartedly rallied behind the government's decision to enter the war. At the 1942 annual meeting of the Northern Baptist Convention, it was resolved that its members should "do anything for the welfare of our country within the full sanction of our individual consciences to achieve a Christian victory and secure for the world a just and lasting peace, regardless of personal cost or sacrifice."

With this war, however, certain segments of American Baptistry opposed the United States' entry into the conflict. Many Baptists of German origin supported Hitler because of his avid nationalism and anticommunism. Others opposed the war for reasons of personal conscience. Harry Emerson Fosdick (1878–1969), for example, had experienced firsthand the horrors of war as a chaplain in World War I and was an energetic pacifist. He used his position as minister at the Riverside Church in New York City to preach neutrality.

After the end of World War II, Baptists again united to support the government's efforts to secure world peace, primarily through the establishment of the United Nations. Similarly, American Baptists assumed a prominent role in the worldwide effort to bring relief to the war-torn nations of Europe; Northern Baptists alone raised over $16,000,000 for this purpose.

On the home front, through both World Wars, Baptists continued to evangelize. Missionary emphasis after the Civil War had shifted from the (by then) fairly well-settled western territories to work among the poor blacks of the South and the immigrant population of the cities. Darwinism had upset the country and the denomination in the early half of the twentieth century. It culminated in the 1920s in the trial of John T. Scopes, a young schoolteacher in Dayton, Tennessee, who violated the state law against teaching evolution; this was an issue that would raise its head again and again throughout the century.

The Depression had forced many urban Baptist churches to close their doors as people fled the cities in search of work or were drafted to fight. After World War II, however, the future looked brighter for the Baptists. A spirit of revivalism was in the air and a new breed of evangelists was taking advantage of modern technological advances—radio, television, and air travel—as well as sophisticated public relations and promotional techniques to spread the Gospel to more and more people. In 1949, when evangelist Billy Graham held his first citywide campaign at the Rose Bowl in Pasadena, California, the tenor of evangelism for the next 30 years was decided.

XIV

"A Return to Normalcy"?

AFTER THE UPHEAVAL AND DEPRIVATIONS OF THE DEPRES-
sion and World War II, there was nothing Americans
wanted more during the postwar years than peace and
stability, a chance to enjoy the prosperity engendered
by the war. Amid the complacency of the 1950s, America's Protestant denominations began to lose ground
steadily in a society that was becoming more and more
secularized, less spiritual, and more materialistic. Religion no longer played a central role in the lives of
most Americans, nor did it generate the passion it had
previously. The majority of Americans still were nominally Christian, but the public profession of their faith
was, for the most part, confined to Sunday services.

The church was no longer the heart of community life; people had too many other things to do with their time. They could go to the movies, take vacations in their cars, or stay at home hypnotized by the black and white flicker of their new television sets.

American Baptists suffered from the complacency of the 1950s along with other denominations, and the growth of powerful, top-heavy denominational organizations contributed to this conservative trend. It also robbed local Baptist churches of much of their highly prized independence. Rachel Caldwell, the wife of a Baptist pastor who ultimately left the denomination, asked,

> How independent, really, is the local Baptist church? What can it do that really matters, without the sanction of the "state office"? Of course, the pressure that is applied for conformity is a great deal less obvious than that of the Roman Catholic hierarchy, but it is just as real, and just as effective. There are still some Baptist churches large enough, and some pastors strong enough, to resist pressure of this type and to maintain a measure of independence—but they are few. By and large, Baptist pastors are expending the greater part of their energies attempting to curry favor with the powers-that-be by fulfilling or even exceeding the expectations of the human beings into whose hands has been given control over Baptist churches.

It appeared that the traditional Baptist pastor was being transformed from spiritual leader and evangelist into an administrator and program director. Gone was the emotional enthusiasm with its grass-roots appeal that once attracted poorer working people to the denomination. At the same time, many churches were losing their wealthier members to the more formally structured Protestant denominations such as the Episcopals. American Baptistry during the 1950s seemed to be moving toward a predominantly homogeneous, middle-class membership, but beneath the placid exterior, change was bubbling up and ready to burst forth.

William Franklin Graham (1918–), better known as Billy Graham, was born and grew up on a dairy farm in North Carolina. After high school his parents urged him to attend Bob Jones College because a friend of the family had gone there; only later did they discover the college was not accredited. The rigid demands of Bob Jones College, plus ill health, caused young Graham to decide to transfer to the Florida Bible Institute, where he developed an interest in preaching. While in Florida he was baptized a Southern Baptist, although his parents were Presbyterians. In 1939 he entered Wheaton College, where he received his B.A. in 1943.

Graham's evangelical career was launched in 1944 when he appeared on a Chicago radio show, "Songs in the Night." The success of his appearance on radio convinced him that he had a future in evangelizing. For the next five years he devoted himself to evangelizing at rallies and small crusades until, in 1949, he led a major crusade in Los Angeles (Pasadena). This crusade was an overwhelming success and set the pattern for Graham's life and for his future crusades. These crusades consisted of a three-week tent meeting campaign with preaching by Graham, song-leading by Cliff Barrows, and gospel singing by George Beverly Shea, culminating in the call to the audience to accept Christ and/or seek counseling. The success of this format immediately was evident, and it launched Graham on an evangelizing campaign that over the years has taken him around the world and, through the medium of television, into the homes of millions. The "phenomenon of Billy Graham did remind the nation that the comforts and gadgets of its benign culture were not satisfying completely the spiritual hunger of many citizens."[1] His emotional preaching and heartfelt appeals reenergized the grass-roots contingency of Baptists and were the forerunners of the kinds of techniques that would be utilized even today. He was one of the first evangelists to realize the power of the new medium, television, and to use it effectively. What was one man's crusade during the 1950s and 1960s was to burgeon into the phenomenon known as televangelism during the 1970s and 1980s. The seed had been sown.

Change also was occurring among the black Baptists, a change that would not only affect their individual religious lives but also the entire political and social structure of the United States. After the Emancipation Proclamation nominally freed the slaves in 1863, the church became the one social institution that blacks could call their own in a society in which they continued to be enslaved socially, politically, and economically. The church was an oasis of comfort, hope, and inspiration in the midst of the grinding hardships of the black person's daily life. It was a place where blacks

[1] Harry J. Carmen, et al. A History of the American People, vol. II, 3rd ed. (New York: Alfred A. Knopf, 1967), p. 827.

could experience the dignity, pride, and sense of fellowship denied them in the white community. Since the church building was often the only available meeting place for large groups in the black community, it became the center of black social and political life as well.

If the church was the heart of the black community, the preacher was its soul and natural leader. As the most visible and respected member of the community, he was looked upon not only as a spiritual guide, but also as family counselor, politician, community spokesperson, and local celebrity. He often was the only black person in the community to command a position of authority and respect in the eyes of whites. As W. E. B. DuBois characterized him in *Souls of Black Folk*:

> The preacher is the most unique personality developed by the Negro on American soil. A leader, a politician, an orator, a "boss," an intriguer, an idealist—all of these he is, and ever too, the centre of a group of men, now twenty, now a thousand in number. The combination of a certain adroitness with deep-seated earnestness, of tact with consummate ability, give him his preeminence, and helps him maintain it.

The black Baptist preacher was and is noted for his oratorical skills and his ability to move his congregation with his words. The sermon is the high point of the black Baptist service, often lasting an hour or more. The entire service tends to be emotionally charged, filled with the sounds of music provided by a large choir and a great deal of "talk-back" and shouting on the part of the congregation.

After the Reconstruction it often fell to the black preacher, because of his influence and education and the respect accorded him, to mediate within the community or between the black and white communities. But until the 1950s little had been achieved in uniting those communities or in furthering the civil rights of blacks; in fact, if anything, blacks had lost ground in the civil rights issue. In 1870 the Fifteenth Amendment passed, prohibiting states from passing laws denying black citizens the vote. In 1875 a Civil Rights Act was passed by Congress, but both of these moves rapidly were overcome by harsh reality. The federal government did little to enforce the Fifteenth Amendment, and in 1883, the Supreme Court declared the Civil Rights Act invalid. A greater blow was to come, however, with the Supreme Court's decision in 1896 in the case of *Plessy vs. Ferguson*, which upheld the idea of segregation so long as separate facilities were provided for blacks that were equal to those provided for whites. This "separate but equal" doctrine was to prevail for the next 58 years.

On May 17, 1954, in the case of *Brown vs. Board of Education of Topeka*, the Supreme Court ruled that racial segregation in public schools was unconstitutional. The Court stated that to separate black school children "from others of similar age and qualifications solely because of their race generates a feeling of inferiority as to their status in the community that may affect their hearts and minds in a way unlikely ever to be undone." A mighty blow had been struck in the battle for desegregation. All the civil rights' cause needed was a leader; and a leader did emerge from that place within the black community where leadership always had resided, the church.

With the legacy of the black preacher to support him, it was only fitting that Dr. Martin Luther King, Jr., (1929-1968) should step forward to become the voice for black Americans in the United States during the 1950s and 1960s. For 14 years before an assassin's bullet tragically cut short his life in 1968, Dr. King was the undisputed spokesman for Christian morality and civil rights. He received a Nobel Peace Prize in 1964 for his efforts.

The son and grandson of preachers, Martin Luther King, Jr., was born and raised in Atlanta, Georgia, in a family and an area steeped in the Southern black tradition. King was an excellent student, attending Morehouse College and Crozer Seminary and receiving his Ph.D. in 1954 from Boston University. While in college King encountered the writings of Mahatma Gandhi and Walter Rauschenbusch and became convinced of the effectiveness of nonviolence in combating social injustice.

Upon graduation, King became a pastor in Montgomery, Alabama, and, faced with the severity of segregation there and spurred by the Supreme Court ruling of 1954, he made the decision to devote himself to social change. King successfully organized a boycott of public buses in Montgomery, a town that previously had forced blacks to sit in the back. He was arrested with 88 others, but he had achieved his goal. This was to set a pattern for King's future protests; in pursuit of desegregation King would be arrested 29 more times. The Montgomery boycott had a second effect as well. King became a national hero, and the publicity his boycott engendered drew supporters from both the black and white communities across the nation.

Blacks and whites alike flocked together in massive rallies and marches led by Dr. King, who preached his message of nonviolence to achieve a "beloved community"—a place where blacks and whites could live in harmony and equality. Like the Social Gospelers and Christian Socialists before him, he maintained that the church should lead the way in the struggle for human and civil rights. As he told a crowd in 1961, at the height of the civil rights movement,

> I am absolutely convinced that men hate each other because they don't know each other. They don't know each other because they are separated from each other. . . . The church has the responsibility to open the channels of communication. . . . God is interested in the freedom of the whole human race, the creation of a society where every man will respect the dignity and worth of human personality.

The following years were filled with marches, sit-ins, pray-ins, boycotts, freedom rides, strikes, demonstrations, and beatings and lynchings. In 1964, after 250,000 people marched on Washington to lobby Congress on behalf of a civil rights bill, President Lyndon Johnson signed the Civil Rights Act of 1964 in law in July.

Although the glory days of the civil rights movement have faded in history, and the stirring oratory of Martin Luther King, Jr., has been silenced by a bullet, others have shouldered King's cause and promoted black interests on the local and national levels. The style of the dynamic Reverend Jesse Jackson (1941–), founder of the Push for Excellence program aimed at motivating poor and minority students to improve their academic skills, echoes that of his former mentor, Dr. King. Jackson stresses the power of education to combat racism in America. "We must raise a new vision for American education," he has said. "We must heal the wounds, the divisions, between black and white."

In 1983 Jackson declared himself a Democratic candidate for the presidency and formed the "Rainbow Coalition," a multiracial support group. Although unsuccessful in 1983, he ran again in 1987. While this bid also was unsuccessful, Jackson has remained influential in both domestic and foreign policy, often using Baptist pulpits to advance his causes.

Martin Luther King, Jr., not only left a legacy for blacks and black preachers who were to follow him, his promotion of nonviolent protest also was eagerly adopted by both blacks and whites—in particular, the "baby boom" children of the 1960s and early 1970s who were rebelling against the "establishment." The civil rights movement and the Vietnam War galvanized a generation of Americans into action, and their activities—protest marches and sit-ins—nearly brought the well-oiled mechanism of American society to a halt.

Similarly, black leaders organized to more effectively run their churches. In 1968 black pastors founded the American Baptist Assembly and the interdenominational National Committee of Negro Churchmen. By the end of the 1970s, the total number of black Baptists in

America was nearly 11,000,000, or one-half the total black population.

America's religious leaders, both black and white, scrambled to respond to the upheavals of the 1960s. The result was a variety of conflicting theological interpretations and doctrinal debates that only added to the general moral confusion. One line of thought adopted by many of the radicals led them to the conclusion that "God is dead." The majority of Americans, no matter what their religious beliefs, were shocked by this notion. While the statement was meant to shake up people, most of the radical theologians did not mean that God *literally* was dead, but that all our old notions about God and man's relationship with God were no longer meaningful or applicable in the modern world. The Reverend Franklin D. Elmer, pastor of Woodside Baptist Church in Flint, Michigan, shed some light on the issue in a thoughtful article that appeared in the American Baptist publication, *Missions*, in 1966:

> We must be ready to admit that the tragedy of religion in our times has resulted because so many of us were brought up in churches and synagogues and mosques and temples where the idea of God we were taught is so limited and inadequate that it was destined only to die, and what we must see in the marvelous, disturbing, revolutionary developments of our time is that, while the inadequate ideas of God are properly dead, a greater idea of God cries out for our acceptance. If the ancient womb of religious faith seems suddenly empty, it is not because the living faith in God that was there has died and been aborted, but rather be-

cause a growing, greater concept of creation and man's place in it has come to birth and is crying out for our acceptance.

By 1970 the United States seemed headed for glory: it had a new conception of God, according to some; civil rights for black citizens had been achieved; and the protests and assassinations of the 1960s were over. This ebullience and self-congratulation would soon be stilled, however, by the conflicts and problems the new decade would hand America—problems that the Baptist denomination would meet with new and innovative solutions.

XV

The Electronic Revival

DURING THE 1970S AMERICANS EXPERIENCED A "CRISIS OF confidence" in their political and moral leadership. Hardly had the last chime of the new decade faded when the high spirits and hope of the 60s began to sour. Almost immediately, it seemed, economic recession set in and the Vietnam War revealed its ugly side. The last straw for many Americans was President Richard M. Nixon's resignation in 1974 under the threat of impeachment for the "Watergate" scandal. Americans who had looked upon the political system as a means of improving society now were gripped with a sense of disillusionment and helplessness. Political activism gave way to general voter apathy, and few issues or candidates could spark the enthusiasm of the vast "silent majority" of Americans.

The generation of Americans that came of age in the 1970s narrowed its scope of interest to areas over which the individual could exercise control: one's own life. Personal advancement and the pursuit of pleasure replaced radical politics and social activism as the favored activities of the young. The members of the "Me" Generation just wanted to be left alone to pursue their own individual goals without interference from their government, their neighbors, or their church.

It is not surprising that the characteristic feature of this new decade would be conservatism in most areas of life—social, political and religious—as many Americans recoiled from the excesses of the 1960s. The new conservatism in religion was a reaction to the sometimes bizarre religious and quasi-religious splinter groups that had sprung up like weeds in the 60s and 70s. These groups ran the gamut from the Eastern influenced Hare Krishna and Transcendental Meditation movements, to the militaristic Unification Church presided over by the Korean industrialist Sun Myung Moon, and the strange philosophy of L. Ron Hubbard and the Scientologists. These groups fell into disfavor under the cloud of horror generated by our own homegrown People's Temple whose members' mass suicide was orchestrated by the demonic Jim Jones.

Many people were likewise disenchanted by the extreme liberalism that had been adopted by many mainstream Protestant denominations in the wake of the 60s. One reaction was a mass exodus away from these denominations and toward the ultra-conservative evangelical churches that had remained firmly grounded in Christian fundamentals throughout the turbulent 60s. There had been a slight flurry of revivalism during the 1920s, but the evangelical emphasis on personal conversion—the so-called "born again" experience—and salvation appealed to the religiously oriented among the "Me" Generation and their embrace of the "old-time religion" began the first major religious revival of the twentieth century.

The election of Jimmy Carter, a self-professed "born-again" Southern Baptist, lay missionary, Sunday school teacher and church deacon, to the presidency in 1976 focused national attention on the evangelical phenomenon. Jimmy Carter was the first Southerner since the Civil War and the first Southern Baptist ever to be elected president of the United States. But what is perhaps more significant is the fact that President Carter openly discussed his "born-again" experience—that spiritual rebirth and commitment to Christ that is one hallmark of the Baptist faith and the symbol of the evangelical revival then taking hold of the nation. With the president openly discussing his religious experience, the average person felt easier in espousing religion and discussing it; in a 1980 Gallup Poll, one in every three Americans claimed to have been "born again."

The revival, which peaked in the late 1980s, has been compared to the Great Awakening of the eighteenth century and the Great Revival of the nineteenth century, with one difference. The revival of the 1970s and 1980s was not, for the most part, conducted in the traditional tent of the evangelical preacher, but rather through the medium of the modern age: television.

While evangelists had taken advantage of both radio
and television since their inceptions, it wasn't until the
1957 New York Crusade of Billy Graham that the vast
potential of television was realized. That was the first
time a religious crusade had been televised in the
United States, and it was a turning point in Graham's
own ministry. During the 1960s Graham became the
voice of the white American conscience, and it increasingly caught the ear of various politicians. This
backfired somewhat in 1973 during the Watergate scandal, when Graham found himself allied too closely to
former President Nixon. Graham quickly recovered,
however, and continued to use television to reach millions of people throughout the world. Television had
vast potential for an evangelist. As Graham noted

> The crowds are larger, the interest deeper, and the
> response is greater than it has ever been. I attribute
> this not only to the power of the Holy Spirit but to
> the fact that the broadcasting media have been
> open to us. I believe one of the greatest factors in
> the religious resurgence in this country has been
> the impact of religious radio and television.

The growth of the religious broadcasting industry
has mushroomed in recent years. Membership in the
National Religious Broadcasters, an association of radio
and television evangelists, increased dramatically from
104 to 900 during the 1970s. By 1980 there were 600
radio stations, 30 television stations, and hundreds of
cable television outlets that broadcast religious programming exclusively. And their numbers were increasing rapidly. The Southern Baptist Radio and

Television Commission was producing over 40 different public service religious programs and was considering expansion into the paid broadcast area. The advantages of such outlets were obvious. As Paul M. Stevens, former president of the commission noted, the commission is "a mission agency, an arm of the church, reaching into areas where churches would be locked out."

A majority of the new "televangelists" adopted the crusading techniques of Billy Graham, and Graham's pioneering efforts generally are recognized by all. However, other new evangelists drew from the medium itself for ideas, utilizing, for example, a talk show format. Many of the evangelists drawn to television were those belonging either to fundamentalist groups or to the charismatic movement. ("Charisma" is defined as "a spiritual gift or talent regarded as divinely granted to a person as a token of grace and favor and exemplified . . . by the power of healing, the gift of tongues, or prophesying.") Among the charismatic evangelists was one who was to have a significant impact on the entire area of religious television: Pat Robertson.

Marion Gordon (Pat) Robertson was born on March 25, 1930, in Lexington, Virginia, a Southern Baptist by birth, heritage, and by ordination. Robertson is the son of a politician—his father served both in the House of Representatives and the Senate. After graduation from Yale Law School in 1955, and while studying for the ministry at the Biblical Seminary of New York, he became interested in charismatics and Pentacostalism. The hallmark of Pentacostalism is its identification of the baptism of the Holy Spirit with speaking in tongues. Pentacostals are convinced that supernatural power—prophecy and healing—are available to Christians from God. Traditionally, Baptists have been more resistant to the charismatic movement than other denominations, having "definite doctrinal scruples" against charismatic theology. However, by the 1980s, charismatics had made some headway within the Southern Baptist church and gained some acceptance.

Upon Robertson's graduation from the seminary, he was offered several jobs. Then during the summer of 1959, he was offered the opportunity to buy into a television station in Portsmouth, Virginia, and his future was settled. The Christian Broadcasting Network began operation on August 3, 1961.

By 1965 CBN was growing; Jay Arlan, who formerly had worked for ABC, became the network program director. The staff had been enlarged to include Jim and Tammy Bakker, a young couple who had been successful evangelists with the Assemblies of God. In September of 1965 the Bakkers began a children's program on CBN called "Come on Over," later renamed the "Jim and Tammy Show." Unfortunately for Robertson, the hiring of this young couple eventually would mean not only the end of much of his own influence in televangelizing but also herald the end of the Electronic Revival itself.

Meanwhile, Robertson also had started the "700 Club" as a means of fund-raising. The idea was to ask 700 listeners to pledge ten dollars a month to support the station. These supporters were called "The 700 Club," a name that later would be adopted by the television show of the same name that was hosted for a time by the Bakkers. The influence of Robertson's television empire spread throughout the 1970s and 1980s, benefiting from the religious enthusiasm that was experiencing a rebirth and, ultimately, giving Robertson the confidence and influence to run for president in 1987. The influence of CBN also had a ripple effect for other televangelists. People were tuning in, not only to CBN, but to other evangelical television shows as well. The televangelists were, at the time, "on a roll."

In 1972 Jim and Tammy Bakker left CBN to start their own network, the PTL Network. PTL, like CBN, was able to exploit the religious fervor of the times and also thrive. For the next 15 years, it flourished and grew. In 1987, however, PTL's "Pearlygate" scandal was exposed. The Electronic Revival came to a screeching halt.

Amid accusations of adultery, homosexuality, extortion, and financial fraud, Jim and Tammy Bakker threw a shadow over all the electronic churches, regardless of denomination, and destroyed any presidential aspirations Pat Robertson might have had. Because many of the televangelists' shows were so similar, the public tended to lump all of them together. A USA Today survey published on April 1, 1987, revealed that over half of those polled felt the scandal had damaged the presidental campaign of Robertson. Most television ministries reported an immediate drop in financial contributions. Although the Bakkers' roots were in the Assemblies of God, which maintains loose Baptist ties, a majority of people believed them to be Baptists and condemned the Baptists generally. Because the Bakkers had started on CBN, many people associated them with that network, which damaged its reputation and influence and that of Robertson. PTL virtually disappeared from the airwaves in 1987, but CBN staggered on for two more years until, at last, in 1989, it changed its name to the Family Channel and dropped much of its religious programming.

What started with the Jim and Tammy Bakker scandal expanded when televangelist Jimmy Swaggart was accused of commiting acts of adultery with a prostitute. Again, the Baptists unjustly received the bad publicity. Swaggart, like the Bakkers, was a member of the Assemblies of God as well, but because his evangelical techniques were similar to those used by the Baptists, Baptists again came under a cloud—as did all evangelical denominations. During these scandals other televangelists tried unsuccessfully to help, the most prominent being Baptist televangelist Jerry Falwell, pastor of the Thomas Road Baptist Church in Lynchburg, Virginia.

During the 1970s and 1980s, Jerry Falwell (1933–) had become the focus of international attention as a preacher, religious educator, and spokesman for conservative political views. A graduate of Lynchburg (Virginia) College and the Baptist Bible College in Springfield, Missouri, Falwell began building his church in Lynchburg immediately after graduation. Focusing on Sunday school organization, he used a number of lay evangelists and buses to create an "aggressive, soul-winning congregation" of, as of 1985, 21,000 members.

During the 1960s Falwell had begun to use his weekly radio and television program, "The Old Time Gospel Hour," to promote his own message of evangelism and his political stances: anti-abortion, traditional morality, strong national defense, and parochial education. Over the years his influence spread and grew. In 1979 he created a political action group, the

Moral Majority, Inc., to further his political and religious philosophy.

Falwell, who describes himself as neither a Republican nor a Democrat but a "noisy Baptist," claimed that evangelicals "are the largest minority in the United States. . . . We're 40 percent of the electorate." The objectives of the Moral Majority's 400,000 members (mostly fundamentalist pastors) was to mold that minority (described by Albert J. Menendez in his *Religion at the Polls* as "the sleeping giant of American politics") into a major moral and political influence in American society. The Moral Majority employed a number of traditional political devices to achieve its goal: voter education and registration drives, lobbying, endorsement and support of candidates, and legal aid for religious issues being debated in court. The Moral Majority's intent, ultimately, was to "recapture America for God" and defeat politically and philosophically what they termed "secularists and humanists."

Interdenominational in its membership, the Moral Majority was a political force to be reckoned with during the 1980s. The group took a stand on various issues: against abortion, gay rights, sex education in schools, pornography, and drug use; and in favor of voluntary prayer in public schools. It also adopted positions on issues that were decidedly secular in nature, opposing the Equal Rights Amendment, limitations in nuclear armament, cuts in defense spending, the new Department of Education, and in favor of support for Israel. Politicians, ever sensitive to the voice of the "people," listened carefully to what the Moral Majority had to say and often voted accordingly.

However, on June 12, 1989, after the end of eight

years of a conservative president who often supported many of the views of the Moral Majority, and having felt the backlash of the Bakker and Swaggart scandals, Jerry Falwell announced that the three-fold aims of the Moral Majority—get people saved, get people baptized, and get people registered to vote—had been accomplished. He disbanded the Moral Majority and returned to his Lynchburg ministry. With the disbanding of the Moral Majority, the Electronic Revival officially was dead.

The message of the Reverend Falwell—and a majority of the televangelists—had been essentially a fundamentalist one. The emphasis of the Electronic Revival was on the absolute authority of the Bible, the divinity of Christ, and the "born-again" experience. The movement had its greatest impact in the South and Midwest, but it also had made serious inroads in the traditional strongholds of theological liberalism everywhere. Between 1965 and 1980, for example, the major Protestant churches (Episcopal, Presbyterian, Methodist, and United Church of Christ) lost 15 percent of their membership. During that same period, membership in the evangelical churches rose more than 25 percent. By 1980 over 30,000,000 Americans claimed to be evangelicals.

The Southern Baptist Convention, the largest of the Baptist conventions, felt the impact of the revival the most. From the beginning the Southern Baptists have tended toward conservatism; however, there always has been a small but vocal fundamentalist group within the convention. With the onset of the Electronic Revival and its fundamentalist emphasis, this group began to seize more and more control within the SBC. One of its most outspoken proponents, televangelist W. A. Criswell, was pastor of the largest Baptist congregation in the nation, the First Baptist Church of Dallas, Texas, past president of the SBC (1968 and 1969), and founder of the Criswell Center for Biblical Studies in Dallas.

Since the mid-1970s the fundamentalists in the Southern Baptist Convention have been engaged in a power struggle with the more moderate conservative leaders. At issue, the moderates feel, is the concept of freedom, a concept basic to the Baptist denomination. During the 1970s fundamentalists led an attack on the quality of biblical instruction in the convention's schools and seminaries. The fundamentalists believed in the inerrancy of the Bible—that every word of the Bible should be taken literally as God's truth—and they felt that the instructors in the SBC's schools were too liberal; they demanded that every teacher accept and teach the absolute authority of the Bible.

At the SBC's annual meeting in 1979, the fundamentalist element scored a victory with the election of Memphis pastor Adrian Rogers to the presidency. Rogers denounced liberal Bible instructors as instruments of the devil, and vowed to purge the convention's seminaries of them.

The fundamentalist element has continued to dominate the SBC through the 1980s and to push their viewpoints. In 1984, for example, the SBC, under fundamentalist control, went on record in opposition to the ordination of women to the ministry. The resolution argued that women are subservient to men because of their responsibility for bringing sin into the world.

One result of this fundamentalist-moderate dispute had been the 1987 formation of the Southern Baptist

Alliance. The SBA is committed to the freedom of the individual to interpret Scripture, freedom of local churches to call and ordain pastors of either sex, a servant model of church leadership, open inquiry in theological education, mission work characterized by evangelism and social justice, the separation of church and state, and, lastly, ecumenism.

While many moderate Baptists joined the Southern Baptist Alliance, an equal number have chosen to remain with the SBC and attempt to wrest control from the fundamentalists. The fundamentalists, on the other hand, view these attempts as an attack by a liberal "neo-orthodoxy" movement. In 1988 the fundamentalists attempted to purge the denomination of anyone who didn't believe that the Bible is completely free from historical error. The attack was led by Houston Appeals Court Judge Paul Pressler, the chief architect of the fundamentalist campaign, and the Reverend Paige Patterson, president of Criswell Center for Biblical Studies. While not successful, they did manage to pass a resolution recommending that lay people submit more fully to the authority of their pastors in, among other things, matters of interpretation of the Bible.

At the end of the 1980s, the Southern Baptist Convention continues to be the strongest of the denominations, with an income of over $3,500,000,000 annually, 37,000 churches, 53 colleges, and 6 seminaries. But as the new decade of the 1990s dawns, it is impossible to predict the outcome of its internal struggles. The Baptist denomination historically has been beset by the conflict between two mutually exclusive desires: the desire for local church autonomy and individual interpretation of the Bible; and the desire for a stronger, centralized organization and a "literalist" view of the Bible. How these two viewpoints will be resolved as a new century looms before us—or *if* they will be resolved—remains to be seen. The old Baptist saw, "where there are two Baptists, there will be three opinions," still holds true. But that is what is to be admired.

The Baptist tradition of independence and the strength to fight for one's beliefs continues even today, as does the Baptist desire to spread those beliefs. And they find, as Jerry Falwell has said, that "Those who quit talking about those sharing their faith and who actually do it soon discover that God will accomplish far more than they ask or dream in the process." Perhaps resolution of their conflicts will be found in the sharing rather than in the talking.

Appendix: Baptist Principles

WITHIN THE BAPTIST DENOMINATION THERE ARE A VARIety of sects and a great deal of diversity. But all Baptists believe

1. in the supremacy of the Bible, rather than in a church or hierarchy;
2. in religious liberty;
3. in the baptism of believers (adult baptism), rather than in infant baptism;
4. in the independence of the local church.

The emphasis on the individual's experience of the Almighty has prevented Baptists from formulating any binding creed or church doctrine. As far as Baptists are concerned, the Bible provides all the spiritual guidance a man may need to come to terms with God, and no dogma created by man could equal the divinely inspired revelations contained in the Scriptures. The Baptists' emphasis on personal conversion as a requirement for church membership has led them to become vigorous promoters of the Gospel. They hold that every church member—every Christian—is an evangelist and is responsible for spreading the Gospel.

Baptists generally hold weekly religious services on Sunday, usually in the morning and the evening. These services customarily are preceded by Sunday school or Bible study classes attended by both children and adults. The Baptist service is marked by a high degree of participation by the congregation. Church members who serve as deacons or hold church office are very active in the service, often reading the lesson and leading the congregation in song and prayer.

The term "Baptist church" is a term of convenience; "denomination" is preferred by most Baptists as each church is an independent, local unit. They do recognize the need for interdependence among churches for purposes of fellowship and the carrying out of certain activities. As a result, a number of local churches may be organized voluntarily into a regional association and/or may belong to a particular convention or conventions.

Bibliography

Armitage, Thomas. *A History of the Baptists*. New York: Bryan, Taylor and Co., 1887.

Armstrong, Ben. *The Electric Church*. Nashville: Thomas Nelson Inc., Publishers, 1979.

Armstrong, O.K., and Marjorie Armstrong. *The Baptists in America*. Garden City, N.Y.: Doubleday and Co., 1979.

Bainten, Roland H. *The Reformation of the Sixteenth Century*. Boston: Beacon Press, 1952.

Berkhofer, Robert F., Jr. *Salvation and the Savage*. New York: Atheneum, 1976.

Brackney, William Henry. *The Baptists*. New York: Greenwood Press, 1988.

Carmen, Harry J., et al. *A History of the American People, Volume II—Since 1865*. New York: Alfred A. Knopf, 1967.

Dickens, A.G. *Reformation and Society in Sixteenth Century Europe*. New York: Harcourt, Brace and World, Inc., 1966.

Falwell, Jerry. *Strength for the Journey*. New York: Simon and Schuster, 1987.

Fogde, Myron J. *Faith of Our Fathers*. Vol. 6. *The Church Goes West*. Washington, D.C.: McGrath Publishing Co., 1977.

Gaustad, Edwin Scott. *The Great Awakening in New England*. Gloucester, Mass.: Peter Smith, 1965.

Gewehr, Wesley M. *The Great Awakening in Virginia*. Gloucester, Mass.: Peter Smith, 1965.

Hamilton, Charles V. *The Black Preacher in America*. New York: William Morrow and Co., Inc., 1972.

Harrell, David Edwin, Jr. *Pat Robertson*. San Francisco: Harper and Row, Publishers, Inc., 1987.

Hillerbrand, Hans J. *The World of the Reformation*. New York: Charles Scribner's Sons, 1973.

Liston, Robert A. *By These Faiths*. New York: Julian Messner, 1977.

Marty, Martin E. *The Righteous Empire*. New York: Dial Press, 1970.

Mead, Frank S. *Handbook of Denominations in the United States*. New York: Abingdon Press, 1965.

Olmstead, Clifton E. *History of Religion in the United States*. Englewood Cliffs, N.J.: Prentice-Hall, Inc., 1960.

Rosten, Leo, ed. *Religions in America*. New York: Simon and Schuster, 1963.

Spence, Hartzell. *The Story of America's Religions*. New York: Holt, Rhinehart and Winston, 1960.

Sweet, William Warren. *Religion in the Development of American Culture, 1765–1840*. New York: Charles Scribner's Sons, 1952.

Thompson, David M. *Nonconformity in the 19th Century*. London: Rutledge and Kegan Paul, 1972.

Torbet, Robert G. *A History of the Baptists*. Valley Forge, Pa.: Judson Press, 1978.

White, B.R. *The English Separatist Tradition from the*

Marion Martyrs to the Pilgrim Fathers. Oxford: Oxford University Press, 1971.

Williams, J. Paul. *What Americans Believe and How They Worship.* New York: Harper and Row, Publishers Inc., 1962.

Wood, James E., Jr., ed. *Baptists and the American Experience.* Valley Forge, Pa.: Judson Press, 1976.

Pamphlets

Baptists of North America, A Fact Book. North American Baptist Fellowship, 1979.

General Baptists. Poplar Bluff, Missouri: General Baptist Home Mission Board, Inc.

Handy, Robert T. *American Baptist Polity: What's Happening and Why.* Historical Commission, Southern Baptist Convention, 1979.

Hodges, Sloan S. *Black Baptists in America and the Origins of Their Conventions.* Washington, D.C.: Progressive National Baptist Convention, Inc.

Magnuson, Norris. *How We Grew.* Evanston, Illinois: Baptist General Conference.

Porter, W. Hubert. *The American Baptist Churches in the U.S.A.* Valley Forge, Pennsylvania, 1979.

Witnessing Together for Christ. North American Baptist Fellowship, 1978.

Articles

Newsweek

Mayer, Allan J., et al. "A Tide of Born-Again Politics." September 15, 1980.

Morganthau, Tom, et al. "The Religion Lobby." July 16, 1979.

Woodward, Kenneth L. and Howard Fineman. "A $1 Million Habit." September 15, 1980.

——————— and Lea Donosky. "Southern Baptists Turning Right?" June 25, 1979.

——————— and Rachel Mark and Jerry Buckley. "Who Was Jesus?" December 24, 1979.

The New York Times
Briggs, Kenneth A. "Christians on Right and Left Take Up Ballot and Cudgel." September 21, 1980.
———————. "Churches Turning to Arms Race as Top Social Issue for the 1980s." March 25, 1979.
———————. "Evangelicals Adding Powerful New Voice to Movement in Churches for Arms Control." January 18, 1979.
———————. "Evangelicals Hear Plea: Politics Now." August 24, 1980.
———————. "Evangelical Preachers Gather to Polish Their Politics." August 21, 1980.
———————. "Fundamentalist Schools Fight Controls." January 26, 1979.
———————. "Liberal Churches Debating Need of Evangelism to Reverse Losses." November 11, 1979.
———————. "The Electronic Church Is Turning More People On." February 10, 1980.
———————. "The Evangelical Boom Keeps Going." December 30, 1979.
———————. "The Influence of Church Leaders in Politics." September 19, 1980.
Clendinen, Dudley. "Rev. Falwell Inspires Evangelical Vote." August 20, 1980.
Dionne, E.J., Jr. "Evangelicals' Vote Is a Major Target." June 29, 1980.
Fiske, Edward B. "Jesse Jackson Builds Up Support in a Drive for Student Discipline." March 4, 1979.
Lewis, Anthony. "Political Religion." September 25, 1980.
———————. "Religion and Politics." September 19, 1980.
Raines, Howell. "Reagan Backs Evangelicals in Their

Political Activities." August 23, 1980.

"Religious Material Gains on Airwaves." February 4, 1978.

Roberts, Steven V. "Evangelicals Press Political Activities." September 29, 1980.

——————. "Fears on Rise About Growing Role of Religion in Election Campaigns." September 24, 1980.

Rule, Sheila. "Black Baptists Are Regrouping for Action." January 13, 1979.

——————. "Blacks Debate Role of Their Modern-Day Churches." July 8, 1979.

Vecsey, George. "Militant Television Preachers Try to Weld Fundamentalist Christians' Political Power." January 21, 1980.

——————. "Southern Baptists Choose a Conservative President." June 13, 1979.

——————. "Baptist Leader Keyed to Bible." June 14, 1979.

——————. "Southern Baptists Divided over Bible Issue." June 10, 1979.

Wall Street Journal
Kaufman, Jonathan. "An Evangelical Revival Is Sweeping the Nation but with Little Effect." July 11, 1980.

INDEX

Abbott, Lyman, 121
abolition, 100, 103; abolition movement in England, 114
Abyssinian Baptist Church, 113, 115
Act of Toleration, 24
Adams, John, 59
Address to the Christian Nobility of the German Nation, 6
adult baptism, 11, 14, 20, 28, 82, 161
Age of Enlightenment, 44
Alabama State Convention, 103
American and Foreign Bible Society, 91
American Baptist Anti-Slavery Convention, 102
American Baptist Assembly, 143
American Baptist Association, 98
"American Baptist Bill of Rights," 131
American Baptist Board of Foreign Missions, 114

American Baptist Churches in the U.S.A., 109, 110, 111; headquarters of, 110, 111
American Baptist Convention *see* American Baptist Churches in the U.S.A.
American Baptist Education Commission *see* American Baptist Education Society
American Baptist Education Society, 88, 89, 109
American Baptist Foreign Mission Society, 108
American Baptist Home Mission Society, 78, 108
American Baptist Missionary Convention, 115
American Baptist Missionary Union, 108, 127
American Baptist Publication Society, 108
American Baptist Publications and Sunday School Society, 91
American Bible Society *see* American Baptist Publica-

tions and Sunday School Society

American Board of Commissioners for Foreign Missions, 81–82

American Colonization Society, 114

American Indian Mission Association, 80

American National Baptist Convention *see* National Baptist Convention, U.S.A. Incorporated

American Revolution, 40, 61, 99, 128

American Sunday School Union, 90

Amish, 13

Anabaptists, 12, 13, 14, 28

Andover Theological Seminary, 81

Anglican Church, 13, 23, 24, 37, 55, 59, 62, 71

Annual Report of the American Baptist Missionary Union, 80

Annuity Board, 111

anti-missionary movement, 51–52, 95, 96

"apostolic succession," 98

Appeal to the Public for Religious Liberty Against the Oppression of the Present Day, 58

Apple Creek Anti-Mission Association, 96

Arlan, Jay, 152

arminianism, 21, 37, 40, 70

Armistice, 127

Assemblies of God, 152, 153, 154

associations, 35, 39, 42, 69, 70, 111

autonomy of local churches, 22, 40, 41, 90, 95, 96, 98, 105, 109, 110, 158, 161

Backus, Isaac, 56, 57, 58, 59, 61

Bakker, Jim and Tammy 152–154, 156

Baldwin, Thomas, 76

Baptist Analytical Repository, 91

Baptist Bible Union, 125

Baptist Committee on Indian Missions, 79

Baptist General Association *see* American Baptist Association

Baptist General Committee, 62, 100

Baptist General Tract Society, 91

Baptist Joint Committee on Public Affairs, xi, 129

Baptist Missionary Magazine, 83

Baptist Missionary Society, 66, 76, 77

Baptist societies, 52, 108, 109

Baptist Standard, 127

Baptist Teacher, The, 92

Baptist Tract Magazine, 91

Baptist World Alliance, 126, 131

Baptist Young People's Union, 109

Baptists, and adult baptism, 11, 14, 20, 28, 82, 161; and abolishionist movement, 100, 103, 114; and autonomy of local churches, 22, 40, 41, 90, 95, 96, 98, 105, 109, 110, 158, 161; and biblical inerrancy, 124, 157; and civil rights, 116, 123, 141–143; and Darwinism, 120; and evangelism, 22, 35, 43–53, 65–74, 138; and evolution, 120; and fundamentalism, 97, 124, 125, 149, 151, 156, 157, 158; and immersion, 20–21, 49, 71, 91; and infant baptism, 12, 14, 20, 28, 29, 49, 57, 61; nd Landmarkism, 97, 98; and laying-on of hands, 40–41, 95; and religious freedom, 16, 17, 18, 19, 22, 23, 24, 25, 27, 29, 30, 31, 35, 36, 39, 52, 55, 56, 57, 58, 59, 60, 61, 62, 63, 126, 130, 131, 161; and separation of church and state, 61, 129, 130, 158; associations, 35, 39, 41–42, 69, 70, 111; education, 40, 85–91; farmer-preachers, 70, 71, 77, 95; first Baptist congregation in England, 17, 30; first English Particular church, 20; first formal, national organization, 82; in Holland and England, 11–25, 66; in America, 27–42, 31, 32, 34, 36, 38; missionary efforts, 40, 51, 66, 76, 77, 78, 79, 80, 81, 82, 83, 84, 87, 91, 92, 95, 96, 114, 115, 116, 123, 125, 126, 127, 128, 132, 144, 158; Northern Baptist Convention, 97, 105, 109, 116, 124–125, 126, 127, 128, 129, 131; publications, 85, 91–92; Southern Baptist Convention, xii, 97, 103, 104, 105, 110, 111, 114, 116, 123, 124, 126, 127, 129, 131, 156, 157, 158; spits and schisms, 48, 50, 51, 93–105, 112, 113, 156–158; state conventions, 98–99; Triennial Convention, 82, 83, 99, 102, 103, 108, 113, 114

"Baptized Believers," 15

Barrows, Cliff, 137
Bates College, 124
"Battle for the Bible," 125
Baylor University, 87
Beecher, Henry Ward, 121
Beissel, John Conrad, 48
believer's baptism *see* adult baptism
Bernard, Richard, 15
Bible, 6, 10, 20, 28, 48, 49, 51, 57, 60, 90, 101, 110, 120, 121, 122, 123, 124, 125, 156, 157, 158, 159, 161
Bible colleges, 89
"Bible religion," 60
biblical inerrancy, 124, 157
Bill of Rights, 61
black Baptists, 49–50, 99, 104, 112, 113, 132, 143, 144, 145; and the Civil Rights movement, 140–144; black conventions, 112–116; first black associations, 50; first black Baptist church, 50; first missionary, 113
Black Death, the, 1
Bloudy Tenent of Persecution, The, 30
Board of Educational Ministries, 109
Board of International Ministries, 109
Board of National Ministries, 109

Boardman, Jr., George D., 123
"born again" experience, the, 149, 156
Boston Female Society for Missionary Purpose, 76
Boyd, Richard H., 116
Bradstreet, Ann, 28
Bristol Baptist Academy, 86
Brown University, 52, 86, 89, 96, 124
Brown vs. Board of Education of Topeka, 140
Browne, Robert "Trouble Church," 12
Brownists, 12
Bucknell University, 87
Bunyan, John, 24

Caldwell, Rachel, 136
Calvin, John, 11
camp meetings, 67, 68
Carey, Lott, 114
Carey, William, 66, 76, 82, 113
Carter, Jimmy, xiii, 149
Character of the Beast, The, 15
charismatic movement, 151, 152
Charles II, 23, 24, 33, 35
Christ *see* Jesus Christ
Christian Broadcasting Network, 152, 153–154
Christian Index, The, 91
"Christian Socialism," 122

Christian Socialists, 142

Christianity and Social Crisis, 122

"Christians Baptized on Profession of Their Faith," 15

Church of England, 11, 12, 13, 30

civil rights, 59, 140, 141, 142, 143, 145; Civil Rights Act of 1875, 140; Civil Rights Act of 1964, 142; Civil Rights Movement, 143

Civil War, 81, 88, 90, 94, 104, 105, 107, 110, 111, 114, 116, 119, 132, 149

Clarendon Code, the, 23

Clarke, John, 32–34

Clarke, William N., 123

Colby College, 87, 124

Colgate University, 87, 124

College of Rhode Island *see* Brown Univversity

Colley, the Reverend, 115

Columbian College *see* George Washington University

Commonwealth, the, 22, 23

Confederate States of America, the, 104

Confession of Faith, the 1612, 19, 20

Confession of Faith, the 1677, 39, 40

Confessions of Nat Turner, The, 101

Congregationalists, 35, 55, 56, 57, 62, 63, 81

Connecticut Constitutional Convention, 63

Canon Law, 6

Conservative Baptist Association, 97

Consolidated American Baptist Missionary Convention, 115

Constitution, the, 60, 61, 93, 112

Continental Congress, the, 58

Conventicle Act, 35

"Cotton Grove Convention," 97

Court of International Justice, 129

Crandell, John, 33

Crane, William, 114

Criswell Center for Biblical Studies, 157, 158

Criswell, W. A., 157

Cromwell, Oliver, 22

Crozer Seminary, 141

Darwin, Charles, 120

Darwinism, 120, 121, 132

Dawson, Joseph M., 130

Declaration of Independence, the, 24

Declaration of Rights, 61

Deism, 44, 45

Denison University, 87

denominationalism, 21, 92, 98, 99

Diet of Worms, 7

Dipper's Dipt, The, 23

Douglas, Stephan A., 94

DuBois, W.E.B., 139

Duncan, S. W., 127

Dungan, Thomas, 38

Dunster, Henry, 34

Dutch Anabaptists *see* Anabaptists

education, 52, 74, 78, 85, 86, 87, 88, 89, 127

Edwards, Jonathan, 45–46

Electronic Revival, The, 147, 152, 153, 156

Elkhorn Association, 69

Elmer, Franklin D., 144

Emancipation Proclaimation, 138

English Civil Wars, 20

English Particular Baptist Society for the Propagation of the Gospel Among the Heathen *see* Baptist Missionary Society

Episcopals, 137, 156

Equal Rights Amendment, 155

Erasmus, 3

evangelical Christianity, 46

evangelizing, 22, 43–52, 65, 66, 74, 76, 78, 79, 81, 82, 132, 133, 137, 138, 149, 162; of Billy Graham, 137–138

evolution, 120, 132

Falwell, Jerry, 154–156, 159

Family Channel, the, 154

farmer-preacher, the, 70, 71, 77, 95

Faunce, William H.P., 123, 124

Featley, Daniel, 23

Federal Council of the Churches of Christ in America *see* National Council of the Churches of Christ in the U.S.A.

feudalism, 2

Fifteenth Amendment, 140

First African Baptist Church of Kingston, 113

Foreign Mission Baptist Convention, 115

Foreign Mission Board, 110–111

Fosdick, Harry Emerson, 132

Franklin, Benjamin, 45

Franklin College, 87

Free Will Baptist Connection, 48, 49, 116

Freedman's Aid Society, 115

Frelinghuysen, Theodore, 45

Friends of Humanity Association, 100

fundamentalists, 97, 124, 125, 149, 151, 156, 157, 158

Furman, Dr. Richard, 82
Furman Academy and Theological Institute see Furman University
Furman University, 87

Gandhi, Mahatma, 141
Garden of Eden, 51
Gazetteer of Illinois, 78
General Assembly of Particular Baptists, 21
General Association of Regular Baptists, 97
General atonement, 17
General Baptists, 19, 20, 21, 24, 37, 41
General Board of the American Baptist Churches in the U.S.A., 109–110
General Mission Convention, 77
General Missionary Convention of the Baptist Denomination see Triennial Convention
General Six Principle Baptists, 35, 39, 41, 95
George Washington University, 83, 87
German Baptist Conference in America, 122
God, 6, 9, 10, 11, 12, 14, 17, 18, 24, 28, 31, 33, 35, 44, 45, 46, 51, 56, 58, 86, 95, 99, 101, 108, 121, 122, 125, 144, 145, 157, 161

Goold, Thomas, 34
Gordon Adoniram Judson, 121
Graham, William Franklin "Billy", 133, 137–138, 150, 151
Granville Literary and Theological Institution see Denison University
Graves, James R., 97
Gray, Thomas R., 101
Great Awakening, the, 43–53, 57, 67, 68, 99, 112, 149
Great Depression, the, 128, 129, 132, 135
Great Revival, the, 65–74, 87, 90, 95, 149
Griffith, Benjamin, 41, 42
Guide to Emigrants, 78

Hare Krishna, 148
Helwys, Joan, 16
Helwys, Thomas, 15, 16–18, 19
Henry VIII, 12
History of Ten Baptist Churches, 71
History of the Rise and Progress of the Baptists in Virginia, A, 68
Hitler, Adolf, 131
Holliman, Ezekiel, 31
Holmes, Obadiah, 33
Holy Roman Empire, 2, 4, 7
Home Mission Board, 110

Hone, Philip, 75
Hubbard, L. Ron, 148
Hutchinson, Ann, 32, 33

Ill Newes From New England, 33
immersion, 20–21, 49, 71, 91
Impartial Inquiries, Respecting the Progress of the Baptist Denomination, 57
Indians, 30, 44, 78, 79, 80, 81
indulgences, selling of, 3, 6
infant baptism, 11, 12, 14, 20, 28, 29, 49, 57, 161
"Influence of Missions on the Temporal Condition of the Heathen," 83

Jackson, Jesse, 143
James I, 13, 17
James II, 24
Jefferson, Thomas, 60, 62
Jesus Christ, 6, 10, 17, 20, 21, 29, 35, 39, 40, 44, 72, 78, 122, 125, 126, 138
"Jim and Tammy Show, The," 152
John the Baptist, 20–21, 72
Johnson, Francis, 13
Johnson, William B., 110
Jones, Jim, 148
Judson, Adoniram, 81, 82, 113, 123
Judson, Ann, 81, 82

Kalamazoo Theological Seminary, 88
Keach, Elias, 39
Ketocton Association, 99
King, Jr., Martin Luther, 116, 123, 141–143
Knox, John, 11

Landmarkism, 97, 98
Latitudinarians, 44, 45
Latter Day Luminary see The Christian Index
Laws, Curtis Lee, 125
laying-on of hands, 40–41, 95
League of Nations, 129
Lee, General Robert E., 104
Leile, George, 113
Leland, John, 59–60, 61, 100
limited atonement *see* predestination
Lincoln, Abraham, 93, 94
Locke, John, 44
London Confession of Faith, 1644, 21
Laury, Robert, 107
Luther, Hans, 4
Luther, Margaret, 4
Luther, Martin, 4–7, 9, 10–11, 17

McCoy, Isaac, 79–80
Madison, James, 60, 61
Madison University *see* Colgate University

Manual-Labor Institute *see* Franklin College
Massachusetts Baptist Missionary Society, 76, 77
Massachusetts Bay Colony, 28, 29, 30, 33, 34, 35
Massachusetts Missionary Magazine, 91
Massee, Jasper C., 124
Mather, Cotton, 36
Mayflower, 112
Mayflower Church Covenant, 12–13
Menendez, Albert J., 155
Mennonites, 13; Waterlander Mennonites, 14, 15, 16
Mercer University, 87
Methodists, xii, 71, 86, 156
Miller, Perry, 32
Ministers and Missionaries Benefit Board, 109
missions and missionaries, 51, 76, 77, 78, 79, 80, 81, 82, 83, 84, 87, 91, 92, 95, 96, 114, 115, 116, 123, 125, 126, 127, 128, 132, 144, 158; missionary societies, 102; first modern Baptist missionary, 113
modernism, 125
modernist movement, 123
"money-based" missions, 51
Moon, Sun Myung, 148
Moral Majority, The, 154–155, 156

Morehouse College, 141
Mount Poney Baptist Church, 60
Mumford, Stephen, 48
Munter, Jan, 15, 30
Murton, John, 17
Myles, John, 34–35

National Baptist Convention of American, Unincorporated, 116
National Baptist Convention, U.S.A. *see* National Baptist Convention, U.S.A., Incorporated
National Baptist Convention, U.S.A., Incorporated, 115, 116, 131
National Baptist Educational Convention *see* National Baptist Convention, U.S.A., Incorporated
National Bicentennial Convention, xi
National Committe of Negro Churchmen, 143
National Council of the Churches of Christ in the U.S.A., 126
National Primitive Baptist Convention of the U.S.A. (formerly Colored Primitive Baptists), 116
National Religious Broadcasters, 150

National Youth Administration, 129
New Deal, the, 129
New Hampshire Confession of Faith (1833, 1853), 97, 111, 124, 125
"New Light" Baptists, 47, 56, 62, 69, 70
New Model Army, 22
New World Movement, 128
Newton Theological Seminary, 87, 89
Nixon, Richard M., 147, 150
Norden, Robert, 38
Northern Baptist Convention, 97, 105, 109, 116, 124–125, 126, 127, 128, 129, 131 see also American Baptist Churches in the U.S.A.
Northern Theological Seminary, 123

Old Landmark Re-Set," "An 97
"Old Light" Baptists, 47, 62, 69, 70 see also Regular Baptists
Old Time Gospel Hour," "The, 154
On the Origin of the Species, 120
Our Little Ones, 92

Palmer, Paul, 38, 48

Panic of 1819, 83
Parker, Daniel, 51
Particular Baptists, 20, 21, 24, 39, 40, 41
Patterson, Paige, 158
"Pearlygate" Scandal, the, 153
Peck, John Mason, 77, 78, 79, 81
Pendleton, James Madison, 97
Penn, William, 38
Pentacostalism, 151
Philadelphia Association of Baptist Churches (Philadelphia Baptist Association), 39–40, 41, 86
Philadelphia Confession of Faith (1742), 40, 41
Pilgrim's Progress, 24
Plessy vs. Ferguson, 140
Powell, Adam Clayton, 113
predestination, 6, 10, 17, 20, 28, 37
Presbyterians, 62, 86, 137, 156
Pressler, Paul, 158
Primitive Baptists, 50, 51, 96, 116
Principles and Inferences Concerning the Visible Church, 14
Progressive National Baptist Convention, 116
Providence Baptist Association of Ohio, 114

PTL Network, the, 153
publication, 85, 91, 92
Publications Board, 111
Puritans, 11, 13, 28, 29, 30, 37, 56, 85
Push for Excellence Program, the, 143

Quakers, 49, 62

"Rainbow Coalition," the, 143
Randall, Benjamin, 48, 49
Rauschenbusch, August, 122
Rauschenbusch, Walter, 121, 122, 123, 141
Reconstruction, 140
Reformation, the, 9, 11
Regular Baptists, 49, 62, 69, 78
Religion at the Polls, 155
religious freedom, 16, 17, 18, 19, 22–25, 27, 29, 30, 31, 35, 36, 39, 52, 55, 56, 57, 58, 59, 60, 61, 62, 63, 112, 126, 130, 131, 157, 161
Restoration, the, 23
Rhode Island Colony, 31, 32, 33, 34, 35, 38
Rice, Luther, 77, 81–83, 86, 87, 91, 95, 98, 113
Richmond African Missionary Society, 114
Robertson, Marion Gordon "Pat", 151–153
Rochester Theological Semi-
nary see Rochester University
Rochester University, 89, 122, 124
Rock Spring Seminary, 87
Rogers, Adrian, 157
Roman Catholic Church, the, xii, 2, 3, 5, 7, 10, 11, 12, 35, 62
Roosevelt, Franklin, 129, 131

Sabbatarians see Seventh-Day Baptists
Sample, Robert, 68
Satan, 51
Schism see splits and schisms
scientific rationalism, 120
Scopes, John T., 132
Screven, William, 38
Se-Baptists, 15
Second Coming of Christ, 121
Second Great Awakening see Great Revival, the
Seeker, 31
"separate but equal" doctrine, 140
"separates," see "New Light" Baptists
separation of church and state, 61, 129, 130, 158
Separatist Movement, 11, 12, 13, 14, 16, 30, 32
Separatists see Separatist Movement

"700 Club," The, 152
Seventh-Day Baptists, 48, 94
Seventh-Day Baptists (German), 48
Shall We Gather at the River?, 107–108
Sharpe, Henry, 113
Shea, George Beverly, 138
Short Declaration of the Mistery of Iniquity, A, 16, 17
"silent majority," the, 148
"sixth principle," the 41, 95
slavery, 93, 94, 99, 100, 102, 103, 104, 105, 108, 110, 112, 113, 114, 138
Smith, Hezekiah, 52
Smyth, John, 11, 13, 14–16, 18, 31
"Social Gospel," the, 122, 123, 142
societies *see* Baptist societies
Somers, Robert, 104
"Songs in the Night," 137
"soul liberty," 31, 124
Souls of Black Folk, 139
Southern Baptist Alliance, 157–158
Southern Baptist Convention, xii, 97, 103, 104, 105, 110, 111, 114, 116, 123, 124, 126, 127, 129, 131, 156, 157, 158; headquarters, 111
Southern Baptist Radio and

Television Commission, 150–151
Spanish-American War, the, 127
splits and schisms, 48, 93, 95, 102, 103, 105, 112, 113
state conventions, 98–99
Stevens, Paul M., 151
Sunday School Board, 111
Sunday School movement, 74, 78, 90, 91, 92, 95, 154, 161
Swaggart, Jimmy, 154, 156

Taylor, John, 71, 96
Taylor, Myron C., 129, 130, 131
"taxation without representation," 55, 58
Teague, Collin, 114
televangelism, 138
televangelists, 151, 156
Tennent, Gilbert, 45
Terrill, Edward, 86
Theology for the Social Gospel, A, 122
Thirteenth Amendment, the, 112
Thoughts on Missions, 96
Tillotson, John, 44
Toleration Act of Connecticut (1743), 47, 62
"traveling churches," 68
Triennial Convention, 82, 83, 99, 102, 103, 108, 113, 114

Truett, George W., xii
Turner, Benjamin, 100
Turner, Nat, 100–102
Two-Seed-in-the-Spirit Pre-
    destination Baptists, 50,
    51, 96

underground railroad, the,
    100
United Baptist Churches of
    Christ, 47
United Church of Christ, 156
United Free Will Baptist
    Church, 116
United Nations, the, 132
University of Chicago, 88,
    89; divinity school, 123
University of Lewisbury see
    Bucknell University
University of Richmond, 87
University of Shanghai, 128

Vassar College, 88
Vietnam War, the, 143, 147
voluntary societies, 77, 98

Warren Baptist Association,
    57, 58, 59
Watchman-Examiner, the,
    125, 127
Watchword, The, 121
Watergate scandal, the, 147,
    150

Waterville College see Colby
    College
Wayland, Francis, 96, 97
Weaver, Rufus W., 130
Webb, Mary, 76
Wheelock, Eleazer, 56
Whitefield, George, 46, 49,
    56
William and Mary, 24
Williams, Roger, 29–32, 79,
    124
Wilson, Woodrow, 128
Winchester, Elhanan, 59
Wittenberg, University of, 5,
    6
Witter, William, 33
Women's American Baptist
    Foreign Mission Societies,
    109
Women's American Baptist
    Home Mission Societies,
    109
Wood, James, xi
Worcester, Noah, 57
World Council of Churches,
    126
World War I, 127, 132
World War II, 132, 135

Young Reaper, The, 92

Zwingli, 11

HIPPOCRENE GREAT RELIGIONS OF THE WORLD
Jim Haskins, General Editor

THE SEVENTH-DAY ADVENTISTS: A History
Anne Devereaux Jordan

Born of "The Great Disappointment" of 1844, the Seventh-Day Adventists have drawn their strength from a continuing optimism that Christ will return. This book recounts how Ellen Gould Harmon White, the prophetess of the movement, and her fellow pioneers, endured great hardships to establish the church and spread its message around the world.

A *"lucid study"*—American Library Association, **Booklist**.

150 pages   ISBN 0-87052-562-X $14.95

THE CATHOLIC CHURCH
Barrie Strauss

A masterful account of the transformation of a first-century Jewish sect into a medieval world power, and into the Catholic Church as we know it today. The author, who lectures on medieval history and culture, focuses on the social and political aspects of Catholicism as an institution, and provides a lucid interpretation of the complex term "Christian."

"Exceptional . . . highly recommended"—American Library Association, **Booklist**.

288 pages   ISBN 0-87052-312-0 $14.95